W9-AAU-915

STUDY GUIDE

updated by

Haroon Khan
Henderson State University

THE CHALLENGE OF DEMOCRACY
Seventh Edition

Kenneth Janda
Northwestern University

Jeffrey M. Berry
Tufts University

Jerry Goldman
Northwestern University

HOUGHTON MIFFLIN COMPANY   BOSTON   NEW YORK

Sponsoring Editor: Mary Dougherty
Development Editor: Katherine Meisenheimer
Editorial Assistant: Tonya Lobato
Manufacturing Coordinator: Marie Barnes

Printed in the U.S.A.

ISBN: 0-618-14479-X

123456789-VG-05 04 03 02 01

Contents

Preface

Designed to accompany the seventh edition of *The Challenge of Democracy*, this study guide will help you succeed in your American Government course whether you are taking it to plan a political career, fulfill a requirement, or become a more politically active citizen.

The study guide is designed to help you succeed by encouraging you to:

1. Synthesize the main points in each chapter in the book.

2. Understand current issues relating to each chapter by focusing on useful textbook pedagogy.

3. Identify the learning objectives in each chapter.

4. Define the key terms used in the book.

5. Test yourself with sample questions to prepare for exams.

6. Research interesting political topics on the Web on your own.

Synthesizing the Main Points

One of the main purposes of the study guide is to summarize the main points of each book chapter. Its purpose is not to replace the textbook but to supplement it. To get the best results, you need to read the textbook and then read the study guide to grasp the key points of each chapter. Pay special attention to the titles and subtitles used in the study guide to identify and understand important key concepts.

Opening Vignettes, Politics in a Changing America, and Compared with What

In the textbook, pay attention to each chapter's opening vignette to understand important events in national politics and then try to relate it to the chapter's core material. Pay special attention to the *Politics in a Changing America* and *Compared with What* boxes in the textbook. *Politics in a Changing America* covers important new issues faced by American government; while the *Compared with What* boxes contrast the United States and other industrialized countries of the world. The study guide will help you synthesize important issues by summarizing material covered in these textbook boxes.

Learning Objectives

Each chapter begins with a list of learning objectives to help you understand the rationale and the goal of each chapter so that you may evaluate for yourself whether you know the material well.

Key Terms

At the end of each chapter in the textbook, there are key terms that you should learn. The study guide defines the terms in an easy-to-understand and abbreviated format so that you can easily comprehend and retain them. The key terms are selected on the basis of their importance to the chapter. If you have a grasp of the terms, you will retain the chapter concepts for a long time.

Sample Questions

The study guide includes both multiple-choice and essay sample exam questions. Using the sample questions, you can test yourself to see if you are familiar with some of the important issues in the chapter. Of course, the sample questions do not include all the possible questions in a chapter, but they are important for your preparation. The essay questions are designed to promote your critical thinking skills and to prepare you for thoughtful participation in classroom discussions. It is important for you to try to participate actively in class discussions. Instructors often assign points for participation in class.

A Guide for Further Research and Information

The study guide also serves as a source for further research and information if you are interested in researching a particular topic relating to American government. Many instructors will require you to write a short research paper. The study guide will direct you toward important sources for beginning your research. The study guide provides a list of useful Web sites for each chapter.

Beyond the Textbook

Also important to your success in the American Government course is keeping abreast of the major events in American and world politics. One way to keep up with such events is to read newspapers on a regular basis. You might try the *New York Times*, the *Washington Post*, or any other major newspaper. In addition, you should try to develop a daily habit of watching the national news on television. You can relate the political issues discussed in the media to the concepts covered in the textbook and thereby construct an informed and intelligent opinion on current political issues.

CHAPTER 1
Freedom, Order, or Equality?

Learning Objectives

After reading this chapter you should be able to

- Define the key terms at the end of the chapter.
- Give practical examples of ways that the values of freedom, order, and equality may conflict.
- Provide a conceptual framework for analyzing government.
- Discuss the three major purposes of government.
- Explain the two dilemmas of government.
- Sketch a continuum of ideological stances on the scope of government, ranging from totalitarianism to anarchism.
- Construct a two-dimensional, fourfold classification of American political ideologies, using the values of freedom, order, and equality.
- Distinguish between liberals and conservatives with regard to their attitudes about the scope and purpose of government.

Freedom, Order, or Equality and the Challenge of Democracy

Chapter 1 explores the meaning of three of the text's five major themes: freedom, order, and equality. These values are important ones in the American political system. They often come into conflict with one another, thus posing a dilemma for people who are forced to choose between competing values. The chapter's opening vignette illustrates the complexities globalization presents in terms of the dilemma of ensuring liberty and at the same time maintaining order. It also raises the question of whether government should allow its citizens complete freedom to do whatever they please and whether government should tax its people progressively. These questions pose dilemmas in terms of the values of freedom, order, and equality. The chapters ahead will focus on the setting, structure, and institutions of American government and the policymaking process; as we proceed, we will see many examples of these conflicting values.

Chapter Overview

The text explains American government and politics in light of these dilemmas and the complexities globalization presents to American government. The authors encourage you to think about what government does and about what it should and should not do. The text also emphasizes the dilemmas that confront governments when they must choose between conflicting values.

The Purposes of Government

Government is the legitimate use of force to control human behavior. Throughout history, government has served three major purposes: (1) maintaining order, including preserving life and protecting property, (2) providing public goods, and (3) promoting equality. Maintaining order, the first purpose, is the oldest and least-contended purpose of government. Most would agree with Thomas Hobbes that the security of civil society is preferable to life in a warlike state of nature. But the question of whether maintaining order requires the government to protect private property finds philosophers such as John Locke and Karl Marx at odds.

The second purpose—providing public goods—leads to questions of just what goods the government ought to provide. Over the years, the scope of American government has expanded considerably, as the government has assumed greater responsibility for providing an array of social benefits. The third purpose of government—promoting equality—is the newest and probably the most controversial purpose of government today. It raises issues about the extent of the government's role in redistributing wealth, regulating social behavior, and providing opportunities.

A Conceptual Framework for Analyzing Government

People often have difficulty understanding American government because they lack a framework to help them organize the facts of politics. The framework supplied in this text distinguishes between the values citizens pursue through government and the *institutional models* that guide them in their efforts to govern themselves democratically. The framework presented here uses five major concepts. The three presented in this chapter—freedom, order, and equality—represent *what* democratic governments try to do. The two remaining concepts concern *how* democratic governments do what they do; governments may behave according to pluralistic or majoritarian models. These models are explained more fully in the next chapter.

The Concepts of Freedom, Order, and Equality

Freedom, as used in this text, is synonymous with *liberty*—that is, the freedom to speak, worship, and so forth. In a narrow sense, *order* consists of preserving life and protecting property, but it may also refer to social order, which prescribes the accepted way of doing things. *Equality* is used to mean several different things: *political equality*, or equality of influence in the political process; *social equality*, or equality in wealth, education, and social status; *equality of opportunity*, or equality in chances for success; and *equality of outcome*, or equality for people in the end. The last concept is connected with the idea of entitlements and requires much more government intervention to sustain than either political equality or equality of opportunity.

Two Dilemmas of Government

Two major dilemmas confront the government today. The first one, the original dilemma, involves tradeoffs between freedom and order. How much freedom are people willing to give up to achieve complete safety? How much insecurity are we willing to tolerate to preserve our personal freedom? The second one, the modern dilemma, deals with the balance between freedom and equality. Should government act to promote equal access by women and African Americans to well-paying jobs, even though this restricts the freedom of their employers?

Ideology and the Scope of Government

Political ideologies provide their adherents with consistent, organized beliefs about government. Each ideology provides a different answer to questions about the scope of government, that is, how far government should go in maintaining order, providing public goods, and promoting equality.

Totalitarianism believes in total control by the government including business, labor, education, religion, sports, and the arts. *Socialists* would control basic industries but might leave room for some private ownership of productive capacities and for the practice of civil liberties. Some socialists practice democratic socialism, which guarantees civil liberties, free elections, and competitive political parties. *Capitalists* favor private ownership of the means of production and no government interference with business. *Libertarians* oppose government action except where absolutely necessary to protect life and property. *Anarchists* oppose all government.

Practical politics in the United States tends to be fought out in the middle ground of this continuum—a place inhabited by conservatives and liberals, who differ on both the scope and the purpose of government action. Liberals favor generous government support for education, wildlife protection, public transportation, and a whole range of social programs. Conservatives believe in smaller government and fewer social programs. In the past, liberals and conservatives have been distinguished by their attitudes toward the scope of government. Today this approach is not quite adequate; ideological divisions among Americans involve not only disagreements over the scope of government but also disagreements about the purposes of government, that is, the degree to which the government should promote freedom, order, and equality.

American Political Ideologies and the Purpose of Government

Liberals and conservatives differ on both of the major value conflicts described in this chapter. By using a two-dimensional classification system that depicts freedom and order on one axis and freedom and equality on the other, it is possible to obtain a more accurate picture of the differences between liberals and conservatives. This scheme yields a fourfold classification of American political ideologies. Under it, those who prefer order to freedom and freedom to equality are *conservatives*. Those who prefer equality to freedom and freedom to order are *liberals*. Those who prefer freedom above the other values are *libertarians*. Those who would give up freedom for either equality or order are called *communitarians*.

Key Terms

globalization	social equality	capitalism
government	equality of opportunity	libertarianism
order	equality of outcome	libertarians
communism	rights	liberals
public goods	totalitarianism	laissez faire
freedom of	police power	anarchism
freedom from	socialism	conservatives
political equality	democratic socialism	communitarians
national sovereignty		

Outlining the Text Chapters

One good way to learn the material in your text is to outline each chapter after you have read it. This will help you understand how a chapter is organized and how its main points fit together. The act of writing out the outline focuses your attention on the material and also reinforces what you have read.

Outlining styles tend to be idiosyncratic: one person might prepare an outline that uses full sentences or long phrases to help recall the substance of sections of the text; another might prefer to rely on brief phrases or key words. For starters though, you will probably want to *use the chapter's main headings and subheadings* as the skeleton for your outline. Then flesh these out by noting the main points within each subheading, and where you think it is useful, add some notes to indicate just how each point is connected to the main heading.

Here is a sample outline of Chapter 1.

Chapter One—Outline

I. The purposes of government
    A. Definition of government: the legitimate use of force within territorial boundaries to control human behavior

   B. Maintain order
      1. Survival
      2. Protecting private property
   C. Provide public goods
      1. Public goods—benefits available to all citizens which are not likely to be produced voluntarily by individuals
      2. Tension between government vs. private business
   D. Promote equality
      1. Economic: redistribute wealth
      2. Social: regulate social behavior
      3. Tension between equality and freedom

II. A conceptual framework for analyzing government
   A. Definition of concept: a generalized idea grouping events, objects, qualities under a common classification or label
   B. Five concepts used in this text
      1. What government tries to do (values)
         a. freedom
         b. order
         c. equality
      2. How governments do it (models)
         a. pluralist
         b. majoritarian

III. The concepts of freedom, order, and equality
   A. Freedom
      1. Freedom of: liberty
      2. Freedom from: immunity, or, as used in this text, equality
   B. Order
      1. Preserving life
      2. Protecting property
      3. Maintaining social order—use of police power
   C. Equality
      1. Political equality
         a. one person, one vote
         b. ability to influence political decisions through wealth or status
      2. Social equality
         a. equality of opportunity: each person has the same chance to succeed in life
         b. equality of outcome
            (1) government redistributes wealth to ensure that economic equality and social equality are achieved
           (2) governmental rights as entitlements

IV. Two dilemmas of government
   A. The original dilemma: freedom vs. order
   B. The modern dilemma: freedom vs. equality

V. Ideology and the scope of government
   A. Definition of ideology: a consistent set of values and beliefs about the proper purpose and scope of government
   B. Continuum of ideologies based on beliefs about governmental scope
      1. Totalitarianism: controls all aspects of behavior in all sectors of society

      2. Socialism
         a. state has broad scope of authority in the economic life of the nation
         b. communism versus democratic socialism
      3. Capitalism
         a. private business operating without government regulations
         b. American capitalism: some regulation of business and direction of overall economy
      4. Libertarianism
         a. opposed to all government action except what is necessary to protect life and property
         b. liberal vs. libertarian
      5. Anarchism
         a. opposed to all government
         b. value freedom
   C. Liberals and conservatives
      1. Liberals
         a. favor broad scope of government in providing public goods
         b. yet reject censorship, regulation of abortion
      2. Conservatives
         a. oppose government role as activist in economy
         b. favor small government
         c. yet favor government regulation of social behavior
      3. Need to look at both scope and purpose of government action

VI. American political ideologies and the purpose of government
   A. Liberals vs. conservatives: the new differences
      1. Conservatives
         a. scope of government: narrow
         b. purpose of government: maintain social order
            (1) coercive power of state may be used to force citizens to be orderly
            (2) preserve traditional patterns of social relations
      2. Liberals
         a. scope of government: broad
         b. purpose of government: promote equality (coercive power of state may be used)
   B. Two-dimensional classification of ideologies
      1. Dimensions
         a. freedom—order
         b. freedom—equality
      2. Four ideological types
         a. libertarians
            (1) value freedom more than order
            (2) value freedom more than equality
         b. liberals
            (1) value freedom more than order
            (2) value equality more than freedom
         c. conservatives
            (1) value freedom more than equality
            (2) value order more than freedom
         d. communitarians
            (1) value equality more than freedom
            (2) value order more than freedom

Research and Resources

This chapter introduces three of the key concepts used to build the analytical framework of the text. Freedom, order, and equality are such important concepts and are so critical to the approach of *The Challenge of Democracy* that you might wish to learn more about these ideas. One way to go about it is to consult an encyclopedia or dictionary, such as the *Encyclopedia Britannica* or *Webster's New World Dictionary*. (Access to *Britannica* is available on-line as a paid service. For a free trial, go to <http://www.eb.com/>.) In these works, you will find a general treatment of the terms. A Libertarian-sponsored site that provides a useful indicator of ideology is www.self-gov.org. You may also want to check on the World's Smallest Political Quiz at www.selectsmart.com; this site allows you to see where you stand on the political spectrum. You may find it helpful to turn to a more specialized work tailored to providing information about subjects as they apply to social or political science.

The following are some useful specialized dictionaries and encyclopedias:

Gould, Julius, and William Kolb, eds. *A Dictionary of the Social Sciences*. Glencoe, IL: Free Press, 1964.

Greenberg, Milton, and Jack C. Plano, eds. *The American Political Dictionary*. 10th ed. New York: Harcourt Brace, 1996.

Kuper, Adam, and Jessica Kuper, eds. *The Social Science Encyclopedia*. 2nd ed. New York: Routledge, 1996.

Shafritz, Jay M. *The HarperCollins Dictionary of American Government and Politics*. New York: Harper Collins, 1992.

Stills, David L., ed. *International Encyclopedia of the Social Sciences*. 17 vols. New York: Macmillan, 1968.

Using Your Knowledge

1. Become familiar with specialized encyclopedias and dictionaries. Look up the terms *equality*, *freedom*, *democracy*, *ideology*, and *pluralism* in some of the works cited above. Compare the material covered in the different sources. Are all these terms included in every work?

2. Visit the Web sites of groups that represent each of the four ideological types discussed in the chapter. At each site, see if you can find statements that illustrate the group's viewpoint on freedom, order, and equality, the key values discussed in this chapter. How well does each group fit into the typology? You may try the Web sites listed here, or at the end of the textbook chapter, or you may try to make your own list of ideologically oriented groups. For libertarians, try <http:www.free-market.net>, for communitarians, <http:www.gwu.edu/~ccps/>, for liberals, <http:www.turnleft.com>, and for conservatives, <http:www.clark.net/pub/jeffd/index.html>.

Sample Exam Questions

Multiple-Choice Questions

(Answers to multiple-choice questions are at the back of this book.)

1. The "I Love You" case offers an example of
   a. a facet of globalization.
   b. an increasing interdependence of citizens.
   c. the challenges the globalization presents to American government.
   d. all of the above.

2. "The legitimate use of force to control human behavior within specified geographic boundaries" is a definition of
   a. politics.
   b. government.
   c. democracy.
   d. totalitarianism.

3. A principle that states that each citizen has one and only one vote is a principle of
   a. political equality.
   b. social equality.
   c. equality of opportunity.
   d. equality of outcome.

4. According to Thomas Hobbes, the main purpose of government is
   a. to distribute ownership of property in an equitable manner.
   b. to protect private property.
   c. to protect the physical security of citizens.
   d. to increase the glory of the Leviathan-like ruler.

5. The political philosopher who first argued that the main purpose of government is to protect the "life, liberty, and property of its citizens" was
   a. Karl Marx.
   b. John Locke.
   c. Thomas Jefferson.
   d. Thomas Hobbes.

6. The modern dilemma of government can be seen in
   a. Oregon's approach to assisted suicide.
   b. Michigan's approach to assisted suicide.
   c. the implementation of the employment provisions of the 1990 Americans with Disabilities Act.
   d. all of the above.

7. Promoting equality of outcome among citizens
   a. has always been a major goal of governments.
   b. is uncontroversial when it involves the redistribution of wealth.
   c. rarely clashes with the value of freedom.
   d. requires more government activity than does promoting equality of opportunity.

8. Governments tax citizens in order to provide benefits and services available to all. Such benefits and services are
   a. a modern innovation unknown in the ancient world.
   b. known as public goods.
   c. the most appropriate use of government power in the eyes of libertarians.
   d. totally unacceptable to conservatives.

9. Socialist states
   a. are all communist.
   b. do not allow private ownership of the means of production.
   c. may guarantee civil liberties.
   d. always feature one-party control of political and social life.

10. Which of the following is an example of the use of the government's police power?
    a. Legislation banning smoking in public buildings
    b. Increased funding for the CIA
    c. Increased funding for the FBI
    d. Legislation sponsoring AIDS research

11. The effort to create gender equity in college athletic programs exemplifies
    a. the modern dilemma of government.
    b. libertarian ideology.
    c. the clash between equality and order.
    d. the conflict between order and freedom.

12. The political ideology that rejects all government action except that which is necessary to protect life and property is called
    a. liberalism.
    b. libertarianism.
    c. capitalism.
    d. anarchism.

13. Scholars measure the extent of globalization in different nations by combining various indicators of
    a. personal contacts across national borders.
    b. international financial transactions.
    c. use of international communication through technology.
    d. use of military force.

14. The modern dilemma of government involves the clash between
    a. equality of opportunity and equality of result.
    b. equality and majoritarian rule.
    c. equality and freedom.
    d. equality and order.

15. In American politics, the fight for the middle ground of government action takes place between
    a. conservatives and liberals.
    b. conservatives and libertarians.
    c. communists and liberals.
    d. socialists and liberals.

16. The term *freedom*, as used in the text, is synonymous with
    a. *equality*.
    b. *liberty*.
    c. *equality of outcome*.
    d. *equality of opportunity*.

17. A person who values order and equality more than freedom would be called a(n)
    a. anarchist.
    b. libertarian.
    c. communitarian.
    d. conservative.

18. All of the following are true *except* that
    a. libertarians value freedom above equality.
    b. liberals value equality more than order.
    c. conservatives value freedom more than equality.
    d. communitarians value freedom more than order.

19. All governments require that citizens
    a. treat one another equally and fair.
    b. serve in the military in some capacity.
    c. give up some freedom in the process of being governed.
    d. pledge allegiance to their flag.

20. The United States opposed efforts to create an International Criminal Court on the following grounds *except*
    a. that U.S. soldiers stationed abroad might be arrested and tried in that court.
    b. that the death penalty might be abolished.
    c. the erosion of U.S. sovereignty.
    d. the loss of U.S. military power.

21. Typically, it is safe to assume that freedom and equality
    a. go hand in hand.
    b. are generally unrelated to each other in most political spheres.
    c. are equally valued by all major ideologies.
    d. conflict when governments enact policies to promote social equality.

22. The violence that disrupted the meeting of the World Trade Organization is an example of
    a. anarchism.
    b. libertarianism.
    c. liberalism.
    d. conservatism.

23. Among the major purposes of government, the newest to be added to the list is
    a. promoting equality.
    b. maintaining order.
    c. doing as little as possible.
    d. providing public goods.

24. Which of the following is a case of government regulation of social behavior to enforce equality?
    a. A state law prohibiting assisted suicide
    b. A state law permitting assisted suicide
    c. A federal law outlawing pornographic material on the Internet
    d. A court decision permitting homosexuals to serve on a local police force

25. Libertarians would be *most* likely to support
    a. a government-sponsored program to combat drug use.
    b. a Mothers Against Drunk Driving campaign to raise the drinking age.
    c. deregulation of the airlines.
    d. a constitutional amendment to prohibit flag burning.

Essay Questions

1. In the spring of 1998, several American college campuses experienced violent protests when restrictions on student use of alcoholic beverages were introduced. Which of the values (freedom, order, or equality) discussed in the chapter would you say are involved in these conflicts? How are they involved? How do the values you have mentioned come into conflict with each other?

2. Why is it important to consider both the scope and the purpose of government action when one classifies ideologies?

3. Explain the key differences between liberals and conservatives in modern American politics.

4. According to the text, the newest major purpose of government is to promote equality. Explain the various meanings of the term *equality*. What aspects of this new purpose of government are controversial in America? Why?

5. What is the responsibility of the United States as a superpower to ensure human rights? What are the problems of enforcing human rights in foreign countries?

CHAPTER 2
Majoritarian or Pluralist Democracy?

Learning Objectives

After reading this chapter you should be able to

- Define the key terms at the end of the chapter.
- Arrange types of governments on a continuum based on the number of rulers they contain.
- Indicate how the symbolic value of democracy has changed over the years.
- List the four principles of procedural democracy.
- Outline the central principles of the substantive view of democracy.
- Point out the differences between the procedural and the substantive views of democracy and indicate the key problems with each.
- Explain why representative democracy has replaced participatory democracy in the modern world.
- Compare and contrast the assumptions and mechanisms of the majoritarian, pluralist, and elite models.
- Discuss the pressures faced by newly democratizing states.
- Make a preliminary attempt to identify the strengths and weaknesses of the majoritarian, pluralist, and elite models as they apply to the American system.

Majoritarianism, Pluralism, and the Challenge of Democracy

In the wake of the Columbine tragedy, the gun control advocates succeeded in passing an initiative in Colorado despite the opposition of the National Rifle Association. This is an example of how a majority could defeat the forces of pluralism. But the forces of pluralism did succeed in blocking gun control legislation in Congress.

Chapter Overview

The Theory of Democratic Government

Forms of government can be arranged on a continuum according to how many people hold power in them—that is, according to whether a government is based on rule by one (an autocracy), by few (an oligarchy), or by many (a democracy).

Historically, rule by the people—democracy—was greeted with scorn; in the modern world, however, most governments try to style themselves as democratic. This chapter provides methods for deciding on the validity of their claims. It defines democracy and tries to show what kind of a democracy America is.

The authors present two different theories of democracy. The first, a procedural theory, emphasizes how decisions are made. It relies on four main principles: universal participation, political equality, majority rule, and responsiveness of representatives to the electorate. Under the requirements of the procedural theory, there need be no protections for minorities. The second theory, a substantive one, pays more attention to the content of what government does. Substantive theorists generally expect the government to protect the basic civil rights and liberties of all, including minorities; some substantive theorists go further and expect the government to ensure various social and economic rights. The difficulty with substantive theory is that it is hard to reach agreement on the scope of government involvement in these social and economic matters. One of the major ideological divisions in the United States revolves around those who believe that the government should be responsible for providing jobs and incomes to the unemployed, and those who believe that government should be responsible for providing only minimal, transitional assistance.

Institutional Models of Democracy

Democracies of today are representative democracies rather than participatory democracies. They require institutional mechanisms to translate public opinion into government policies. These institutional mechanisms might be designed to tie governmental policies closely to the will of the *majority*, or they may be structured to allow *groups* of citizens to defend their interests before government.

The classic model of democracy is the *majoritarian model*. It assumes a population of knowledgeable voters who willingly go to the polls to vote on issues and to select candidates whom they have decided, through rational evaluation, will best represent them. The main tools of majoritarian democracy are elections, referenda, and initiatives. (Though public opinion in America supports national referenda, referenda and initiatives are available only at the state and local level.) While proponents of majoritarian democracy point to the stability of public opinion and to Americans' desires to become more involved in politics, critics argue that majoritarian assumptions do not correspond very well to American political reality. For example, in the United States, citizens are not well informed, and voter turnout is low.

A second model, the *pluralist model*, better reflects the limited knowledge and participation of the real electorate. It envisions democratic politics taking place within an arena of interest groups. This model relies on open access that allows individuals to organize into groups to press their claims on multiple centers of governmental power (Congress, state legislatures, bureaucratic agencies, and so on).

A third model, *elite theory*, which is also discussed in this chapter, is more of an antidemocratic theory. Elite theory maintains that democracy is a sham, since power is really in the hands of a small number of individuals who control all governmental decisions and manipulate the political agenda. Yet, in American politics, it seems that although a small group of people may have a big impact, the groups that are effective change with each issue. This observation undermines the elite theory.

Democracy and Globalization

No government actually lives up fully to the standards of either the pluralist or the majoritarian model, but some nations come close enough to be called democracies.

Democracies have been rare throughout history, but recently, with the fall of communism, many more countries, including Russia, have been trying to democratize. Their struggles show that the transition to democracy is not easy and may be complicated by economic difficulties and ethnic tensions.

Does the United States qualify as a democracy? The authors contend that it does, and in this chapter and throughout the text, they explore which model best describes American democracy. They argue that the pluralist model more closely conforms to the American system than either the elitist or majoritarian models.

Key Terms

autocracy	majority rule	majoritarian model of democracy
oligarchy	participatory democracy	deliberative democracy
democracy	representative democracy	interest group
procedural democratic theory	responsiveness	pluralist model of democracy
universal participation	substantive democratic theory	elite theory
political equality	minority rights	democratization

Research and Resources

The first chapter of this guide introduced you to specialized encyclopedias and dictionaries. Those fairly massive works are not updated very frequently, and they are geared to provide an introduction to or an overview of a subject. If you need in-depth information, you will probably want to start by looking for books on your subject. For that, begin with the card catalog or computer terminal that lets you search for books in your library. The emerging electronic "information superhighway" now makes it possible for many students to look beyond the confines of their own campus and visit the card catalogs of many of the finest libraries in the world, using the Internet. When you discover books on your topic that are not in your library, check with your librarian to see if you can arrange for an interlibrary loan.

Since the process of writing, editing, and publishing books takes months, you will not usually find the most up-to-date information in books. So, you will want to supplement your trip to the card catalog or on-line catalog with a visit to the area of the library where periodical indexes are kept. If you learned how to write term papers in high school, you may be familiar with the *Readers' Guide to Periodical Literature*. It helps you locate articles in magazines of general popular interest. The subjects it includes range from "abalone" to "zoom lenses." Since the *Readers' Guide* provides general coverage of so many areas, it is not the best source for specialized works in a particular field. For help in locating specialized periodical literature in political science, try the three excellent indexes listed here. These indexes have long been available in paper form, and many college and university libraries now have them available in convenient CD-ROM form as well. Check with your librarian.

1. *ABC POL SCI*. Santa Barbara, CA: ABC-Clio. This index specializes in publications on political science and government. It includes foreign and non-English-language materials and is a little harder to use than either of the next two. The subject index in the back of this work gives you reference numbers for articles. The articles are listed by reference number in the front of the volume.

2. *Public Affairs Information Service (PAIS)*. New York: Public Affairs Information Service. This index includes books, government publications, and reports of public and private agencies, in addition to periodical articles on government, economic and social conditions, and business and international relations. Articles are indexed by subject.

3. *Social Sciences Index (SSI)*. New York: H. W. Wilson Co. This index covers English-language periodicals in the social sciences, including anthropology, economics, environmental sciences, geography, law criminology, planning, public administration, psychology, social aspects of medicine, and sociology, as well as political science. Articles are indexed by subject and by author.

4. *Lexis-Nexis*, a division of Reed Elsevier, provides on-line access to a wide variety of news articles about government, politics, business, and law. Many colleges have either the full version available or its somewhat scaled-down sibling, *Academic Universe*.

Using Your Knowledge

1. Check with your college library to see which paper and on-line indexes mentioned above are available for your use. Select at least two of the following, *SSI*, *ABC POL SCI*, *PAIS*, or *Lexis-Nexis*, and look for works on democracy published in the last year. After you have located "democracy" in the indexes, browse through the list of titles, narrow your focus, and prepare a short bibliography on some aspect of democracy. (Examples might include "Democracy in the Third World," "Democracy in Eastern Europe," "Pluralist Democracy," "Democracy in America," and "Measuring Democracy Throughout the World.")

2. Here are some Web sites devoted to "democracy": Democracy 2000 at <http://www.democracy 2000.org/>, the Direct Democracy Center, <http://www.primenet.com/%7Econduit>; and New

Democracy, <http://members.aol.com/newdem/>. Visit each Web site and describe the form of democracy advocated there. In particular, note whether each site supports a form of democracy that is more pluralist or majoritarian?

Sample Exam Questions

Multiple-Choice Questions

1. Proposition 209 offers an example of
   a. majoritarian democracy.
   b. pluralist democracy.
   c. elitism.
   d. substantive democracy.

2. An election that allows the voters to make a choice on a policy issue is called a(n)
   a. referendum.
   b. initiative.
   c. recall.
   d. public opinion poll.

3. New England town meetings are examples of
   a. representative democracy.
   b. elitism.
   c. participatory democracy.
   d. populism.

4. The procedural theory of democracy upholds all of the following principles *except*
   a. political equality.
   b. majority rule.
   c. universal participation.
   d. protection of minorities.

5. The principle of responsiveness
   a. protects minority rights.
   b. is unnecessary in representative democracy.
   c. would disallow prayer in public schools.
   d. requires elected officials to do what the people want.

6. The substantive theory of democracy
   a. gives rise to disagreements about what is really required for democracy.
   b. supports civil rights only.
   c. supports civil and social rights only.
   d. always supports civil, social, and economic rights.

7. Americans differ considerably from the citizens of most other western democracies in their view of the government's responsibility to
   a. provide social services.
   b. ensure order.
   c. maintain law.
   d. provide security.

8. The majoritarian model of democrat government
   a. offers protection for minority rights.
   b. relies on a relatively passive citizenry.
   c. expects citizens to have a high degree of knowledge.
   d. fits well with the behavior of voters in America.

9. The form of democracy suitable to small societies where people rule themselves is called
   a. representative democracy.
   b. indirect democracy.
   c. participatory democracy.
   d. procedural democracy.

10. A society that is ruled by a few people is called a(n)
    a. autocracy.
    b. polyarchy.
    c. oligarchy.
    d. democracy.

11. The pluralist theory of democracy
    a. is basically the same as majoritarian theory in its assumptions about citizens.
    b. sees democracy operating through the activities of groups.
    c. rejects decentralization as undemocratic.
    d. works better in unitary rather than federal systems.

12. Which of the following is *not* among the watchwords associated with pluralist democracy?
    a. One person, one vote
    b. Divided authority
    c. Decentralization
    d. Open access

13. Which of the following pieces of evidence would opponents of a system of national referenda be *most* likely to use to support their case?
    a. Polls showing the public's views on the desirability of referenda
    b. Polls demonstrating people's knowledge about political issues
    c. Polls showing the public's views on the desirability of leaving decision making to their elected representatives
    d. Discussions of the technical feasibility of such a system

14. The type of democracy most compatible with minority rule is
    a. procedural.
    b. direct.
    c. pluralist.
    d. centralized.

15. Elite theory differs from pluralist theory by defining government conflict in terms of
    a. many minorities thwarting the majority.
    b. one durable minority ruling the majority.
    c. interchangeable minorities and special interests dominating specific policy areas.
    d. substantive rather than procedural democracy.

16. A model of government that places a high value on participation by people organized in groups is
    a. elitism.
    b. substantive democracy.
    c. pluralism.
    d. majoritarianism.

17. Elite theory portrays American government as a(n)
    a. oligarchy.
    b. autocracy.
    c. polyarchy.
    d. majoritarian democracy.

18. According to the text, American democracy is *best* described as
    a. elitist.
    b. pluralist.
    c. majoritarian.
    d. substantive.

19. The idea that government responsiveness comes through mass political participation is fundamental to the
    a. substantive theory of democracy.
    b. majoritarian theory of democracy.
    c. pluralist theory of democracy.
    d. elitist theory.

20. The argument that affirmative action is desirable because it promotes representation of diverse groups mirroring the diversity of society is *most* consistent with
    a. elitism.
    b. majoritarianism.
    c. segregationism.
    d. pluralism.

21. A system in which formal institutions and practices of constitutional democracy are present but a ruler, party, or regime severely limits competition is called
    a. directed democracy.
    b. contested sovereignty.
    c. ambiguous democracy.
    d. majoritarian democracy.

22. Universal participation, political equality, and majority rule are principles that
    a. define democracy in procedural democratic theory.
    b. define democracy in substantive democratic theory.
    c. conflict with one another and are impossible to achieve together in the same system.
    d. were incorporated into the U.S. Constitution from the beginning.

23. Democratic governments and processes
    a. guarantee correct decisions.
    b. always protect minority rights.
    c. reject unlimited majority rule.
    d. may not necessarily result in desirable policies.

24. The principle of majority rule conflicts *most* directly with which of the following?
    a. Popular sovereignty
    b. Minority rights
    c. A sense of community identity
    d. Governmental responsiveness

25. According to the text, if governments were arrayed on a continuum, the type of government one would find at the opposite end from autocracy would be
    a. oligarchy.
    b. monarchy.
    c. aristocracy.
    d. democracy.

Essay Questions

1. "Representative democracy is not democratic and should be replaced by participatory democracy." Advance arguments for and against this proposition. Which side is more convincing? Why?

2. Explain how the principles of procedural democracy may threaten liberty.

3. Establishing democracy in the world is a long-term goal of the United States. To what extent should the United States pursue this goal?

4. What are the problems faced by the new democracies of the world? What role should the United States play in helping the newly democratic countries?

5. The text asks: "Which is better: a government that is highly responsive to public opinion on all matters, or one that responds deliberately to organized groups that argue their cases effectively?" Outline the pros and cons of each side of this issue. Which side do you find more convincing? Why?

CHAPTER 3
The Constitution

Learning Objectives

After reading this chapter you should be able to

- Define the key terms at the end of the chapter.
- Analyze the conflict between Britain and the colonies.
- Explain how the colonial and revolutionary experiences shaped America's first try at self-government under the Articles of Confederation.
- Account for the failure of the Articles of Confederation.
- Outline the main features of the Virginia and New Jersey plans and describe the major compromises made by the delegates to the Constitutional Convention.
- Explain the four basic principles underlying the Constitution and show how they reflected the Americans' revolutionary values.
- Discuss the way the issue of slavery arose at the Constitutional Convention.
- Summarize the provisions of each article of the Constitution.
- Describe the formal and informal processes of constitutional change.
- Explain how the promise of a bill of rights was used to ensure ratification of the Constitution.

The Constitution and the Challenge of Democracy

The Watergate crisis, discussed in this chapter's opening vignette, seriously tested the constitutional order designed by the nation's founders, and the constitutional order passed the test with flying colors. It had been designed to reconcile order with freedom, a problem this text calls the original dilemma. The founders recognized the need for government to protect life, liberty, and property, but they had just won their freedom from Britain, and they feared that a new, remote national government might threaten the very freedoms it was established to protect. In their first attempt to create a government under the Articles of Confederation, they gave too little power to the national government. As a result, that government was unable to maintain order. In drawing up the Constitution, the founders looked for ways to give adequate power to the national government while still safeguarding freedom. To achieve this end, they designed four principal tools: the separation of powers, checks and balances, republicanism, and federalism.

Although the founders paid a great deal of attention to the conflict between order and freedom, they were not particularly concerned with the tension between freedom and equality—after all, as the authors of the text point out, that is a modern dilemma. The eighteenth-century document accepted slavery and left the qualifications for voting up to the states. As a result, African Americans, women, and poor people were all excluded from the political process. Only later did these matters of social and political equality become issues.

With respect to the text's second theme—the conflict between pluralist and majoritarian models—this chapter points out that the constitutional order was designed to be pluralist. The founders were afraid of majority rule and relied on factions' counteracting one another—a mechanism characteristic of pluralism.

Chapter Overview

The American Constitution is very brief, very old, and very durable. Although it was itself the ultimate product of a revolution, it has provided a remarkably stable political framework, able to accommodate America's growth and development from a collection of eighteenth-century agrarian states to a twentieth-century superpower. The document's own historical roots grew out of three experiences: colonialism, revolution, and the failure of the Articles of Confederation.

The Revolutionary Roots of the Constitution

The colonists in America expected to enjoy the rights of Englishmen. These rights included not being taxed without being represented in the government. The colonists had their own colonial legislature, which legislated for them on domestic matters, but Britain controlled overseas trade and foreign affairs. When Britain decided to tax the colonists to pay administrative (including defense) costs, the colonists viewed it as a violation of their right not to be taxed without having representation. The colonies began to unite in their opposition to British policies, and in 1776, colonial delegates to the Second Continental Congress declared America's independence from Britain. The Declaration of Independence set out the philosophical justification for the break. Following arguments developed by English philosopher John Locke nearly a century earlier, Thomas Jefferson asserted that the colonists had inalienable rights to life, liberty, and the pursuit of happiness; that people created governments to protect those rights; and that when a government threatened those rights, the people had the right to alter or abolish it. The declaration then listed a long series of charges against the king to show how he had violated the colonists' rights, thus justifying their revolution.

From Revolution to Confederation

The Declaration of Independence and the Revolutionary War established that the American colonies would not be governed by England, but they did not determine how the new nation would be governed. In their first effort to structure a system of government, the newly independent Americans established a republic under the Articles of Confederation. This system created a loose confederation that protected the sovereignty of the individual states. The Articles had several major failings: the central government had no power to tax or to regulate interstate or foreign commerce; there was no real executive to direct the government; and any amendment to the Articles required unanimous consent of the state legislatures. These flaws crippled the new government. Events such as Shays' Rebellion soon underscored the need for a new form of government better equipped to maintain order.

From Confederation to Constitution

The delegates charged to "revise" the Articles quickly agreed that more than minor changes were required. They debated the Virginia Plan, which included among its provisions a strong central government with three branches (legislative, executive, judicial); a two-chamber legislature, which could negate state laws (with representation in proportion to taxes paid or in proportion to the free population); and an executive selected by the legislature and limited to one term. Much of the Virginia Plan was adopted, but only after challenges and amendments. In particular, small states believed that the Virginia Plan did not represent their interests. One small-state challenge came in the form of the New Jersey Plan, which gave less power to the central government and proposed a one-chamber legislature in which states would have equal representation.

To solve the conflict between the big and small states over representation, the delegates fashioned the Great (or "Connecticut") Compromise. Under this arrangement, each state would have equal representation in the Senate and representation according to its population in the House of Representatives. Revenue bills would have to originate in the House.

Additional compromises resulted in a one-person executive who would serve a four-year term and be eligible for reelection. This executive (the president) would be selected by an electoral college, in which states would have the same number of votes as they have in the two chambers of Congress combined.

The Final Product

The Constitution begins with a preamble that creates a people, explains the reasons for the Constitution, articulates the goals of the government, and fashions that government. The Constitution is based on four major principles: republicanism, in which power resides in the people and is exercised by their representatives; federalism, which divides power between the national and state governments; separation of powers, which is the assignment of the law-making, law-enforcing, and law-interpreting functions of government to independent legislative, executive, and judicial branches in order to prevent the monopoly of power by one branch; and checks and balances, which gives each branch some power to limit the actions of the other branches. The first of the seven articles of the Constitution establishes a bicameral (two-chambered) legislature endowed with eighteen enumerated powers, including the powers to tax and spend and to regulate interstate commerce. The "elastic clause" (Article I, Section 8) gives Congress the powers necessary to effect its enumerated powers.

The office of the executive is created in Article II, which describes the qualifications required for the presidency and specifies the process for selecting the president by the electoral college. Article II also lists procedures for removing the president by impeachment and describes the powers of the presidency.

Article III establishes a Supreme Court and specifies the method of appointing and removing judges. Most of the details of the judicial stem are left up to Congress.

The remaining articles provide that each state must give full faith and credit to the actions of the other states. They also outline the procedure for admitting new states, establish the procedure for amending the Constitution, and specify that the Constitution is the supreme law of the land.

Some authors argue that the framers of the Constitution may have been motivated in part by economic issues, but their most important source of motivation was the inability of the national and state governments under the Articles of Confederation to maintain order. Their desire to create a system that would maintain order was so strong that the framers readily compromised to allow the institution of slavery to continue.

Selling the Constitution

The Constitution had to be approved by nine states before it could take effect. The campaigns for and against ratification were intense, and the votes taken in several states were quite close. For people to accept the Constitution, its supporters had to allay fears of governmental threats to freedom. The *Federalist* papers explained and defended the principles of the Constitution. Their authors argued that factions (pluralism), the mechanism of representation, and the application of checks and balances could be used to prevent tyranny. Finally, the promise to add a bill of rights placing certain fundamental rights beyond the bounds of government interference helped win support.

Constitutional Change

The Constitution provides a mechanism for amending it, including two means of proposing amendments (by a convention or by a two-thirds vote in each house of Congress) and two means of ratifying proposed amendments (by three-fourths of the states, either through their legislatures or through state conventions). The amendment process requires extraordinary majorities and makes formal constitutional change fairly difficult.

The Constitution changes in other ways, however. Through judicial interpretation, the courts often give new meaning to constitutional provisions and thus make the Constitution adaptable to a changing world. Changing political practice has also altered the way the Constitution is applied.

An Evaluation of the Constitution

The Constitution was successfully designed to provide the order lacking under the Articles of Confederation while at the same time protecting the freedom of individuals. However, social and political inequality—the issues that give rise to what is referred to in Chapter 1 as the modern dilemma—were not yet thought of as important goals of government. Only after the Civil War were amendments added that dealt with the issues of inequality.

The Constitution established a republican structure of government, in which the government rests on the consent of the governed. It was not the intent of the framers to create a democracy that rested on majority rule, however. Thus, from the outset, the Constitution was more pluralist than majoritarian.

Key Terms

Declaration of Independence	judicial branch	enumerated powers
social-contract theory	New Jersey Plan	necessary and proper clause
republic	Great Compromise	implied powers
confederation	republicanism	judicial review
Articles of Confederation	federalism	supremacy clause
Virginia Plan	separation of powers	Bill of Rights
legislative branch	checks and balances	extraordinary majorities
executive branch		

Research and Resources

The framers of the Constitution produced a remarkably durable government framework. The system they designed combined strength and flexibility. Over the years, it has evolved and been adapted to fit the needs of the times. As circumstances change, decision makers fashion responses to new situations. The Constitution itself may be silent on a particular matter at issue. Yet, often policymakers will look to the founders for guidance. What exactly did they have in mind when they established a certain constitutional provision? Can a new course of action be justified by showing that it accords with the spirit of the Constitution?

What sources help reveal the intentions of the framers? Generally, good researchers try to rely on primary material—that is, on firsthand accounts, written by the participants themselves, or on official records of the debates—rather than on secondary material such as interpretations offered by analysts not party to the Constitutional Convention. You have already encountered one important primary source of information about the intentions of the founders. The *Federalist* papers, written by "Publius," were in fact coauthored by James Madison, the "father of the Constitution." (They are available on-line at <http://www.augur.demon.co.uk/federalist-papers/index.htm>; a searchable version may be found at <http://lcweb2.loc.gov/const/fedquery.html>.) The work was written for a polemical purpose—namely, to put the best face possible on the Constitution in order to sell it to New Yorkers. Still, it has proved a valuable guide to understanding how Madison, at least, expected the Constitution to operate.

Another important primary source information on the Constitution and the framers' ideas about it is Max Farrand, ed., *The Records of the Federal Convention of 1787* (New Haven, CT: Yale University Press, 1937). In this work, Farrand has compiled, in chronological order, the *Journal* (essentially the minutes of the meetings), as well as the notes made by many of the participants, including James Madison, Alexander Hamilton, Rufus King, James McHenry, George Mason, and others. There is an extensive index at the end of the fourth volume. On-line, see the Web site of the Constitution Society at <http://www.constitution.org> which carries an extensive collection of documents about the founding, including James Madison's Notes on the Debates of the Federal Convention. (See <http://www.constitution.org/cs_found.htm>. This site also contains a selection of constitutions from around the world. Information about the lives of the framers may be found on the Web site of the National Archives and Records Administration at <http://dolley.nara.gov/exhall/charter/constitution/confathers.html>.

For an in-depth modern source on the Constitution and its development, you may wish to consult Leonard W. Levy, *Encyclopedia of the American Constitution with Supplement* (New York: Macmillan, 1997).

Using Your Knowledge

1. Using *The Records of the Federal Convention of 1787*, or the National Archives and Records Administration Web site mentioned above, select a delegate to the Convention and imagine yourself in his position. What are his main concerns? What interests does he seem to represent? Why? What role does he play in the Convention? What do you know about his subsequent career?

2. Chapter 3 emphasizes the ways in which the original dilemma of freedom versus order influenced the design of the Constitution. What if a constitutional convention were called today, and—like the one in 1787—simply decided to start anew? Speculate on what such a meeting might produce by outlining your own version of a modern constitution tailored for the United States today. Explain how your constitution would deal with both the original dilemma of freedom versus order and the modern dilemma of freedom versus equality.

3. America's two most important political documents, the Constitution and the Declaration of Independence, both deal with the dilemma of freedom versus order. Read both documents and compare and contrast the ways they address that issue.

4. Obtain a copy of the constitution of a foreign nation and a copy of the constitution of one of the states of the United States (try <http://www.constitution.org/cons/natlcons.htm>). Compare these to the U.S. Constitution. What similarities and/or differences do you find?

Sample Exam Questions

Multiple-Choice Questions

1. All of the following helped shape the design of the Constitution *except*
    a. the revolution against Britain.
    b. George Washington's warning against entangling alliances.
    c. the nation's experience under the Articles of Confederation.
    d. America's colonial past.

2. The First Continental Congress was convened because of the conflict between the
    a. American desire for liberty and the British desire for order.
    b. British desire for liberty and the American desire for liberty from taxation.
    c. American desire for equality and the British desire for superiority.
    d. American desire for equality and the British desire for freedom.

3. In his Treatise on Civil Government, John Locke embraced all of the following *except*
    a. natural rights.
    b. government by consent of the governed.
    c. the abolition of slavery in the colonies.
    d. the right of resistance or revolution.

4. The Declaration of Independence justified America's rebellion based on
    a. the separation of powers.
    b. the separate-but-equal doctrine.
    c. natural rights and contract theory.
    d. divine right and the theory of concurrent majorities.

5. Which of the following was among the reasons the revolutionaries tried to win the support of Catholic colonists?
   a. Catholics constituted a very large proportion of the colonial population.
   b. Toleration of Catholics was a key feature of the revolutionaries' respect for religious freedom.
   c. Support from the Catholic population in the colonies might help the revolutionaries get help from France.
   d. Irish Catholics in Boston had started the Boston Tea Party.

6. A government in which power is exercised by representatives who are responsible to the governed is called a
   a. republic.
   b. democracy. *k: to majority*
   c. federation.
   d. plutocracy.

7. The division of power between national and state governments is called
   a. separation of powers.
   b. checks and balances.
   c. eminent domain.
   d. federalism.

8. The founders felt they had to replace the Articles of Confederation with the Constitution because
   a. order was breaking down.
   b. freedom was limited by the central government.
   c. they wanted to construct a majoritarian democracy.
   d. the Articles promoted inequality by allowing slavery.

9. Under the Constitution, the president is commander-in-chief of the military, but Congress has the power to declare war and authorize funds necessary to pay the armed forces. This is an example of
   a. division of powers.
   b. checks and balances.
   c. federalism.
   d. republicanism.

10. The fact that Congress has two chambers, one in which states have equal representation and one in which state representation is based on population, is a result of
    a. the Virginia Plan.
    b. the New Jersey Plan.
    c. the Connecticut Compromise.
    d. the Federalist Plan.

11. The New Jersey Plan would have
    a. apportioned representation according to taxes paid.
    b. accentuated the inequalities among states.
    c. amended rather than replaced the government under the Articles.
    d. vested enormous power in the executive.

12. The Virginia Plan
    a. allowed the national legislature to nullify state laws.
    b. provided for the president to be chosen by an electoral college.
    c. was supported by small states.
    d. promoted political equality by giving access to power to the poor.

13. The compromise on the presidency provided for
    a. a two-term limit on presidential tenure.
    b. direct election by the people.
    c. presidential election and impeachment by the people.
    d. the House to choose a president if no candidate received a majority in the electoral college.

14. The principle that assigns lawmaking, law enforcing, and law interpreting to different branches of government is
    a. republicanism.
    b. federalism.
    c. separation of powers.
    d. checks and balances.

15. The three-fifths clause
    a. counted each slave as three-fifths of a person for the purpose of taxation but not representation.
    b. counted each slave as three-fifths of a person for the purpose of representation but not taxation.
    c. gave each slave a vote worth three-fifths as much as his master's vote.
    d. gave disproportionate influence in presidential elections to white men in slave states.

16. The principle that gives each branch of government some scrutiny and control over the other branches is
    a. republicanism.
    b. federalism.
    c. separation of powers.
    d. checks and balances.

17. The *Federalist* papers did all of the following *except*
    a. provide a rationale for pluralism.
    b. argue for the necessity of a bill of rights.
    c. support a strong central government.
    d. point out how checks and balances would limit tyranny.

18. Hamilton opposed the addition of a bill of rights because
    a. he wanted to increase the power of the national government over the states.
    b. a bill of rights would limit the power of the states.
    c. he believed that specifying areas where the government could not intervene might imply that it had the right to intervene in areas not listed.
    d. he was an antifederalist who wanted the Constitution to be defeated.

19. Under the American Constitution, change has never come about as a result of
    a. judicial review.
    b. calling a national convention.
    c. an amendment ratified by state conventions.
    d. evolving political practice.

20. Many countries followed the U.S. Constitution's principles of civil liberties *except*
    a. Romania.
    b. Slovenia.
    c. Lithuania.
    d. Armenia.

21. The major premise of the Declaration of Independence was that
    a. a government's responsibility is to preserve order.
    b. Great Britain never had a legitimate claim over the people in the colonies.
    c. people have a right to revolt when they determine that the government is destructive of their rights.
    d. only direct democracy is consistent with government for the American colonies.

22. The Constitution was designed primarily to
    a. advance economic equality.
    b. advance social equality.
    c. create a democracy based on majority rule.
    d. strike a balance between freedom and order.

23. In 1992, a long-forgotten amendment originally submitted to the states in 1789 was ratified. That amendment, the twenty-seventh,
    a. prohibits flag burning.
    b. guarantees the right to privacy.
    c. prohibits legislators from voting themselves immediate pay raises.
    d. requires the government to balance the budget.

24. Which of the following was *never* an issue within the Constitutional Convention of 1787?
    a. Balancing the desire for pure democracy with the interest in a republican form of government
    b. Finding an agreeable way to represent populations of slave and free states
    c. Finding an agreeable way to represent large states and small states
    d. Reconciling the views of those who favored a strong national government with those wanting a looser confederation

25. Success of democracy in former communist countries will depend on several factors including
    a. the courage to resist past totalitarian practices.
    b. the willingness to make important adjustments to national institutions.
    c. perhaps a measure of good luck.
    d. all of the above.

Essay Questions

1. The text states that the Watergate affair tested constitutional order in the United States and that "it passed with high honors." Write an essay in which you explain how Watergate tested the American political system. What features of the constitutional structure contributed to a peaceful resolution of the crisis?

2. Does the design of the Constitution promote majoritarian or pluralist politics? Explain your answer.

3. Describe the campaign to have the Constitution ratified. How did the Bill of Rights fit into that campaign?

4. Should the U.S. Constitution be a model for the newly democratic countries? What potential problems will these countries face?

5. Do you consider the British system to be more flexible than the U.S. system? What are the advantages and disadvantages of each system?

CHAPTER 4
Federalism

Learning Objectives

After reading this chapter you should be able to

- Define the key terms at the end of the chapter.
- Explain why the founders adopted a federal system.
- Contrast the two competing views of federalism.
- Describe the tools used by the national government to extend its power over the states.
- Distinguish between categorical grants and block grants.
- Trace the shifting balance of power between national and state governments in the nineteenth and twentieth centuries.
- Discuss the difficulties associated with reshaping the federal system.
- Contrast the approaches taken by Presidents Nixon through Clinton in their efforts to reshape federalism.
- List the main types of local government units.
- Outline the advantages and disadvantages of the federal system.

Federalism and the Challenge of Democracy

Chapter 3 explained that the founders relied on a number of devices to protect freedom while providing order. One of these devices was federalism, a system that divided power between the national and state governments. Although the Constitution does specify the powers that belong to each level of government, the national government has used the elastic clause and historical circumstances to increase its power considerably. The election of 2000 illustrates the two elements of the working of federalism: the respective sovereignty of national and state governments and the power of the Supreme Court to overturn the decision of the state court.

Chapter Overview

Theories of Federalism

The federal form of government was the founders' solution to the problem of making one nation out of thirteen independent states. Federalism is a form of political organization in which two or more governments exercise power and authority over the same people and territory. Federalism helped solve the problem of how to cope with diversity.

Representations of American Federalism

The founding of the United States gave rise to competing approaches to federalism. The first, dual federalism, emphasizes the following four points: (1) the national government may rule only by using powers specifically listed in the Constitution, (2) the national government has only limited purposes, (3) national and state governments are sovereign in their own spheres, and (4) the relationships between the state and national governments are marked by tension. This view places importance on states' rights—the state and national governments are as distinct and separate as the layers of a cake.

The second approach, cooperative federalism, highlights the following three elements: (1) national and state agencies perform joint functions, not just separate ones; (2) they routinely share power; and (3) power in government is fragmented rather than concentrated at one level. The functions of the state and national governments are intermixed, like the different flavors in a marble cake. Cooperative federalists stress the Constitution's elastic clause, which has allowed the national government to stretch its powers.

Cooperative federalism has been associated with liberalism and the tendency to centralize power in the national government. Conservatives have tended to favor returning power to the states.

The Dynamics of Federalism

Although the Constitution defines the powers of the national and state governments, the actual balance of power between them has often been a matter of historical circumstances. Constitutional amendments have led to some change in the balance, but so have legislation and judicial interpretation.

Through legislation, the national government forbade various practices used by the states to disenfranchise African Americans. Through judicial interpretation, the Supreme Court forced state and local governments to meet demands they were otherwise unwilling or unable to meet. The Court extended the Bill of Rights to the states, outlawing segregated schools, providing minimum standards of due process, and forcing the reapportionment of legislative districts according to the "one person, one vote" principle. Recently, the Court has shifted the balance back to the states with the exception of the decision involving the 2000 presidential election.

The national government also uses financial incentives to extend its power over the states. Grants give the national government substantial power to induce states to comply with national standards. Categorical grants, targeted for special purposes, leave recipients with relatively little choice about how to spend the money; block grants, awarded for more general purposes, allow the recipient more discretion.

The Developing Concept of Federalism

Successive generations have changed the balance of power between the national and state governments. In the early nineteenth century, in *McCulloch v. Maryland,* the Supreme Court backed an interpretation of federalism that favored a strong national government. The states' rights issue later stood at the heart of the dispute between the North and South that led to the Civil War. In the 1930s, the power of the national government expanded enormously as President Franklin Roosevelt tried to cope with the emergency created by the Great Depression. The Supreme Court still held fast to a dual-federalist approach, however, and struck down many New Deal programs. By the late 1930s, the Court had altered its views about the balance of power between the national and state governments and sustained acts that expanded the power of the national government. The general welfare became an accepted concern of the national government.

In the 1950s and 1960s, the national government assumed a new role in promoting social equality by combating racism and poverty. As a result, the national government expanded its power, and the states' freedom of action decreased. The Supreme Court outlawed racially segregated schools, and Congress passed the Civil Rights Acts of 1964, prohibiting racial discrimination in areas regulated by the states. During the War on Poverty of the 1960s, the government became involved in a huge number and variety of programs. The clear boundaries that dual federalists sought between the national and state governments were nowhere to be found.

From New Federalism to New-Age Federalism

Calls to reform the complicated system began with Nixon's New Federalism, which relied primarily on block grants to shift the balance of power between the nation and the states. President Carter, too, campaigned on a promise to reduce the size and cost of the national government, as did his immediate successors, Presidents

Reagan and Bush. Their efforts to reshape the federal system relied on program consolidation, budget cuts, and freedom for state officials in administering programs.

Although the national government now provides states with a smaller fraction of the funds they need, it still tries to tell state and local governments what to do. Since the mid-1960s, Congress has used pre-emption to take over functions that were previously left to the states. Pre-emption works through mandates (which force states to undertake activities) and restraints (which forbid states to exercise certain powers). It results in shifting costs to states for nationally imposed policies. The Republican-led 104th Congress passed legislation to limit the national government's ability to pass unfunded mandates on to the states.

Other Governments in the Federal System

The American system includes more than the one national and fifty state governments. Some eighty-seven thousand other governments also exercise power and authority over people living within the boundaries of the United States. Among them are municipal governments, county governments, school districts, and special districts.

Theoretically, one advantage of having so many governments is that they allow citizens the opportunity to decide their own fate in their local community, which they know intimately. However, people are less likely to participate in local elections than in national votes. A decentralized federal system gives more points of access to groups representing special interests. The multiplicity of governments also permits experimentation with new ideas and flexibility in responding to the diversity of conditions that exist around the country. But some argue that the profusion of governments makes government less comprehensible to the ordinary citizen.

Contemporary Federalism and the Dilemmas of Democracy

In reality, the expectations of neither the liberals nor the conservatives have been fully met as federalism has evolved over the last decade. Greater professionalization in the state governments has made them more like "big governments," ready to take an active role in solving problems. Sometimes this has meant that states have been willing to set higher standards than the national government for welfare, product safety and the like.

Most conservatives would like to return power to the states and reduce the role of the national government. But as the national government worked to reduce its size and trim the tax burden it imposes on citizens, state governments grew and raised their taxes. Both liberals and conservatives now sound the theme of smaller, more efficient government.

Federalism and Globalization

Some scholars suggest that the world is moving towards diminished state sovereignty and increased interstate linkages. The creation of the European Union demonstrates the fact that the forces of federalism can overcome long-held religious, ethnic, linguistic, and cultural divisions.

Key Terms

federalism	grant-in-aid	mandate
dual federalism	categorical grant	restraint
states' rights	formula grant	municipal government
implied powers	project grant	county government
cooperative federalism	block grant	school district
elastic clause	nullification	special district
commerce clause	pre-emption	home rule

Research and Resources

You will find considerable information about American states in one of the most commonly available reference works, *The World Almanac and Book of Facts*. On-line, the Information Please Almanac at <http://www.infoplease.com> offers profiles of each state but is less helpful as a source of comparative data. Links to the Web sites of individual states may be found at <http://www.yahoo.com/Government/U_S_ _ Government/U_S_ _States/>. Two pages at *Project Vote Smart* also provide comparable information for all states. One organizes material by state (<http://www.vote-smart.org/ state/>), and the other organizes material by category (for example, governor, legislature, statistics; <http://www.vote-smart.org/state/Topics/>). The National Council of State Legislatures exists to serve state legislators by providing information, research on critical state issues, publications, meetings and seminars, a legislative information database, a voice in Washington, D.C., and staff to assist legislators and their staff in solving problems. The NSCL's on-line presence can serve you in your quest for information about state governments. See <http://www.ncsl.org/>.

To get a sense of "states as laboratories," visit the Government Online Web site at <http://www.gol.org/>. There you will find descriptions of innovative practices adopted by individual states in more than a dozen policy areas including transportation, education, human services, technology, and public safety.

Using Your Knowledge

1. Pick up the current volume of The World Almanac and Book of Facts, and look up the word states to get a sense of the kind of comparative data available on a state-by-state basis. Next, select four states in different parts of the country, and profile each of them using a common set of characteristics you suspect might have political importance. (For example, you might look at net migration, ethnicity of population, indicators that show the importance of industry or agriculture, military contracts, and so on.)

2. Tour Web sites of several state governments. Compare and contrast the types of information they make available.

3. Check out the Government Online Web site mentioned above. Select a policy area and examine the innovative policy solutions offered in at least two different states.

Getting Involved

One of the great advantages of pluralist democracy is that it provides lots of opportunities for you to get involved. If you would like to learn more about the inner workings of government, you need not go to Washington, D.C. With over eighty thousand governments in our system, there are bound to be possibilities for internship right in your own backyard in state and local government. It is not possible to provide detailed information for all fifty states, but here are a few examples of what is out there.

The Citizens' Forum on Self-Government offers an eight-week program for interns to work on matters concerned with the structure and function of state and local governments. There is a small stipend. The application deadline is in mid-April. For further information, contact the Intern Coordinator, Citizens' Forum/National Municipal League, 55 West 44th Street, New York, NY 10036; or call (212) 730-7930.

Like their Washington counterpart, several state legislatures have internships available. In Indiana, for example, the Democratic and Republican caucuses in each house of the state legislature offer paid internships to students who help during the legislative session. In addition, the caucuses sometimes help place internship candidates in positions with interest groups or think tanks in the area. Some other states offering internships include Florida, Illinois, Michigan, Minnesota, Montana, New York, and Rhode Island.

Finally, many cities (including Oakland, California; Phoenix, Arizona; New York City; Detroit; and Los Angeles) offer internship possibilities. Try calling the local government personnel office in your own area to find out what is available near you.

Sample Exam Questions

Multiple-Choice Questions

1. The concept of "states' rights" is most commonly associated with
   a. marble-cake federalism.
   b. cooperative federalism.
   c. layer-cake federalism.
   d. new federalism.

2. Cooperative federalism emphasizes
   a. a readily expandable elastic clause.
   b. the layer-cake metaphor.
   c. states' rights.
   d. the Tenth Amendment as a limit on the national government.

3. Home rule means that cities
   a. are allowed to enact and enforce their own legislation.
   b. are ruled by the state, which exercises direct authority over all matters.
   c. are ruled directly by the White House, which has primary jurisdiction over them.
   d. act in narrowly defined administrative areas only.

4. Dual federalism accepts all of the following principles *except*
   a. the claim that the national government rules by enumerated powers only.
   b. recognition of the dynamic purposes of the national government.
   c. separate spheres of sovereignty for national and state governments.
   d. a relationship between national and state governments characterized by tension.

5. The quality of being supreme in power or authority is
   a. sovereignty.
   b. cooperative federalism.
   c. new federalism.
   d. dual federalism.

6. The elastic or necessary and proper clause of the Constitution has been used by cooperative federalists to
   a. limit the power of the national government.
   b. enhance the power of state governments.
   c. promote interaction between the levels of government.
   d. protect state sovereignty.

7. The balance of power between the national and state governments has been affected by
   a. constitutional amendments.
   b. judicial interpretation.
   c. federal grant money.
   d. all of the above.

8. Categorical grants
   a. leave little discretion to recipient governments.
   b. never require state or local governments to match funds.
   c. are awarded on the basis of politically neutral formulas.
   d. do all of the above.

9. The Supreme Court decided that the Violence against Women Act of 2000 violated what provision of the Constitution?
   a. Commerce clause of the 14th Amendment
   b. National sovereignty of the 10th Amendment
   c. Equal protection of the 14th Amendment
   d. None of the above

10. The Supreme Court case that upheld the doctrines of national supremacy and implied powers was
    a. *Marbury v. Madison.*
    b. *McCulloch v. Maryland.*
    c. *United States v. Butler.*
    d. *Hammer v. Dagenhart.*

11. The mode of national-state interaction during the New Deal
    a. marked the triumph of layer-cake federalism.
    b. reflected laissez-faire philosophy.
    c. was consistently rejected by the Supreme Court.
    d. led Americans to look to the national government for solutions to problems.

12. In *Brown v. Board of Education*, the Supreme Court
    a. increased the freedom of the states to regulate school attendance.
    b. promoted equality by outlawing segregation in public schools.
    c. upheld the role of the states in maintaining the traditional social order.
    d. promoted majoritarian democracy by protecting voting rights.

13. When the national government imposes requirements on state and local governments without providing financial support to meet the requirements, the practice is called
    a. an unfunded mandate.
    b. new federalism.
    c. cooperative federalism.
    d. none of the above.

14. President Reagan's approach to federalism emphasized
    a. block grants and budget cuts.
    b. block grants and revenue sharing.
    c. a principled reconsideration of government functions.
    d. a strict ideologically based division of powers between national and state governments.

15. Which of the following is *not* generally advanced as an argument in favor of federalism?
    a. States, acting as laboratories of democracy, may experiment with new policies.
    b. People are free to "vote with their feet" by choosing the state whose laws suit them best.
    c. Federalism acts to promote racial equality.
    d. Federalism recognizes the diversity of conditions in different states.

16. The authors note that the main constitutional authority for the Voting Rights Act of 1965 came primarily from
    a. the elastic clause.
    b. the Fifteenth Amendment.
    c. the Twenty-Fourth Amendment.
    d. none of the above.

17. Pre-emption has involved the use of
    a. mandates.
    b. restraints.
    c. cost shifting to states.
    d. all of the above.

18. In 2000, the Supreme Court struck down Massachusetts' law that withheld state business from companies that did business with Myanmar (formerly Burma) on the basis of the Constitution's
    a. supremacy clause.
    b. national sovereignty clause.
    c. states' rights clause.
    d. national supremacy clause.

19. The idea that a state could declare an act of the national government null and void was called
    a. the legislative veto.
    b. judicial review.
    c. nullification.
    d. separation of powers.

20. Which of the following amendments did the *least* to change the balance of power between the national and state governments?
    a. The Fourteenth Amendment
    b. The Sixteenth Amendment
    c. The Seventeenth Amendment
    d. The Twenty-Seventh Amendment

21. Throughout American history, the Supreme Court's interpretation of federalism
    a. has always been broad.
    b. has always been narrow.
    c. has varied considerably.
    d. has had little impact on relations between the national and state governments.

22. The 1967 Age Discrimination in Employment Act stripped states of their power to establish compulsory retirement ages for their employees. This is an example of
    a. cooperative federalism.
    b. judicial interpretation.
    c. pre-emption.
    d. dual federalism.

23. The Tenth Amendment to the Constitution asserts that
    a. Congress shall make no law prohibiting the free exercise of religion.
    b. slavery shall be outlawed in the United States.
    c. no state shall deny any person due process of law.
    d. the powers not explicitly granted to the national government are reserved for the states or the people.

24. States that refuse to lower their blood alcohol level standard by 2004 stand to lose
    a. millions of dollars in categorical grants.
    b. millions of dollars in highway construction money.
    c. millions of dollars in project grants.
    d. millions of dollars in education money.

25. The Supreme Court's decision in *United States v. Lopez* suggests a more narrow construction of which source of national governmental power?
    a. Commerce clause
    b. Unfunded mandates
    c. Revenue sharing
    d. The "full faith and credit" clause

Essay Questions

1. Explain the two competing views of federalism.

2. Discuss the factors that have led to the growth of the national government's power.

3. The Supreme Court spoke clearly in 1987: direct congressional control of the drinking age would be unconstitutional. Explain how, despite this decision, there came to be a single drinking age nationwide. What key points about federalism are exemplified by the drinking age issue?

4. Do you consider the EU to be a federation or a confederation? Justify your answer.

5. Based on the 2000 election controversy, assess the dispute between national and state sovereignty.

CHAPTER 5
Public Opinion and Political Socialization

Learning Objectives

After reading this chapter you should be able to

- Define the key terms at the end of chapter.
- Contrast the majoritarian and plural models of democracy with respect to their assumptions about public opinion.
- Explain what is meant by the shape and stability of the distribution of public opinion.
- List the agents of early political socialization, and describe their impact.
- List the major sources of continuing political socialization among adults.
- Show how social or demographic characteristics (such as education, income, ethnicity, region, religion, and so forth) are linked to political values.
- Analyze how the two-dimensional typology of political ideology presented in Chapter 1 applies to the actual distribution of political opinions among Americans.

Public Opinion and Political Socialization and the Challenge of Democracy

This chapter's opening vignette contrasts public attitudes toward punishment in the United States and Saudi Arabia. To maintain a high degree of order and a low crime rate, the Saudis behead, flog, and dismember offenders. Although a majority of Americans favor capital punishment, American public opinion would not tolerate the kinds of grisly punishments accepted as a matter of course by the Saudi public. The pardon of Washington in the rape case drew widespread support for allowing the convicted prisoners to have DNA tests, according to a Gallup Poll in 2000. Public opinion thus places boundaries on allowable types of public policy.

Yet, American attitudes themselves do change over time. Specifically, Americans are more likely to favor capital punishment during periods when the social order is threatened (for instance, by war, foreign subversion, or crime).

An examination of people's opinions on the clashes between freedom and order and freedom and equality shows that the public really does divide itself into the four ideological categories suggested in Chapter 1. Furthermore, the four groups differ in terms of their socioeconomic and demographic characteristics.

The nature of public opinion is particularly important to the distinction between the pluralist and majoritarian models of democracy. These models differ in their assumptions about the role of public opinion. Majoritarians depend on an informed public with stable opinions acting to clearly guide public policy. They believe government should do what the public wants. Pluralists, on the other hand, do not expect the general public to demonstrate much knowledge or display stable or consistent opinions. Consequently, pluralists doubt that majority opinion can provide a good guide for public policy. Instead, they depend on interested and knowledgeable subgroups to compete in an open process to achieve public policy goals.

Opinion research certainly shows that the majoritarian assumptions about knowledge do not describe the public as a whole. Yet, lack of knowledge itself does not prevent people from expressing an opinion on an issue. However, when knowledge and interest concerning an issue both are low, public opinion is likely to be changing and unstable. Groups that are highly interested in an issue do have more opportunity to make an impact, yet such groups are often directly opposed by other groups. Politically powerful groups divide on what they want government to do. As a result, politicians have a great deal of leeway in deciding what policies to pursue. And as the opening vignette points out, although the government tends to react to public opinion, it does not always do what the people want.

Chapter Overview

Public Opinion and Models of Democracy

Public opinion is defined as the collective attitude of the citizenry on a given issue. Pluralists and majoritarians differ on the role of public opinion in a democracy. Majoritarians believe that government should do what the majority of the public wants. Pluralists think the opinion of the general public is not very clear or settled but that subgroups may have very well-developed opinions that must be allowed to be openly asserted if democracy is to function.

Modern polling techniques developed over the last fifty years now make it possible to find out what the people's attitudes are—and to predict presidential elections. One of the oldest polls in the nation is the Gallup Poll.

The Distribution of Public Opinion

In analyzing public opinion, researchers pay attention to its distribution, including both the shape (normal, skewed, bimodal) and stability of the distribution over time.

Political Socialization

Public opinion is rooted in political values, which are in turn produced through a process of political socialization. Early political socialization comes from one's family and school, as well as peer and community groups. Among adults, peer groups and mass media, especially television, play a particularly influential role in the ongoing process of socialization.

Social Groups and Political Values

People with similar backgrounds often share various learning experiences, and they tend to develop similar political opinions. Background factors generally believed to affect political opinions include education, income, region, ethnicity, religion, and gender. Historical context also influences people's political views. At the turn of the century, for example, there were major differences between the newer immigrants from Ireland, Italy, and Eastern Europe and the more established Americans of British stock. Today, this ethnic division is less important than a new ethnicity based on race, which links African Americans, Latinos, and other minorities that tend to share common political attitudes.

From Values to Ideology

Surveys show relatively little use of ideological labels by voters when they discuss politics; but, most voters are willing to place themselves on a liberal-to-conservative continuum. Nonetheless, they often lack the consistent values and beliefs about the scope and purpose of government that characterize truly ideological thinking.

When people are asked to describe liberals and conservatives, they employ two different themes: first, they associate liberals with change and conservatives with preservation of traditional values (freedom versus order); second, they link liberals with more interventionist government (freedom versus equality). When people are asked about their own attitudes on these issues, they separate into four groups, not two.

This suggests that the liberal-conservative ideological framework oversimplifies matters, that ideology is not one-dimensional. By examining where they stand on two areas of conflict—freedom versus order and freedom versus equality—Americans may be divided into four ideological types: liberals, conservatives, communitarians, and libertarians. (This is the same typology that was introduced in Chapter 1.) People with similar socioeconomic and demographic characteristics also often share the same ideological outlook. Minorities and people with less education and low incomes are often communitarians. Libertarians tend to have more education and higher incomes. Conservatives are more common in the Midwest, and liberals are more common in the Northeast.

The Process of Forming Political Opinions

A minority of citizens form their political opinions around ideology; most citizens rely on other factors. This chapter considers four of them: self-interest, political information, political leadership, and opinion schemas.

Although self-interest is often the dominant influence on opinions about economic matters and matters of social equality, there are many issues for which personal benefit is not a factor. Citizens often have difficulty forming opinions in these areas, and they may change opinions easily. Americans have many sources of political information, yet their political knowledge and level of political sophistication tend to be low. Despite their ignorance on political matters, Americans are still willing to express opinions on issues. While researchers suggest that individual opinions are based on low information and are often highly changeable, they also suggest that collective opinion changes less readily. The basic institutions of American government and the positions of the two major political parties on prominent issues are known to at least half the people.

Citizens rely on opinion schemas—networks of organized knowledge and beliefs that guide the processing of political information on a particular subject. Personal opinion schemes often parallel individuals' ideological orientation.

Finally, political leaders also influence the formation of public opinion. Favorable or unfavorable evaluations of a politician may shape public opinion concerning the politician's proposals. Furthermore, experts and television news commentators also serve as very effective shapers of public opinion.

Key Terms

public opinion	stable distribution	socioeconomic status
skewed distribution	political socialization	self-interest principle
bimodal distribution	"old" ethnicity	opinion schema
normal distribution	"new" ethnicity	

Research and Resources

No doubt you are already familiar with a number of public opinion polls. Newspapers, magazines, and television news broadcasts often present information gathered through public opinion polling. Well-known polls include those done by Harris and Roper organizations, ABC News/*New York Times* polls, CBS News/*Washington Post* polls, and, of course, the Gallup Poll. Data from these polls is often publicly available. The Gallup Organization, for example, puts out a monthly publication giving the results of its surveys. Periodically, these surveys are indexed and bound in permanent volumes, which can be found in the reference sections of most college libraries. Gallup also maintains a Web site at <http://www.gallup.com/> where you will be able to find current poll data, information on trends in presidential popularity, and poll results dating back to 1996.

Another excellent source of data on public opinion are the National Election Studies which may be found on-line at <http://www.umich.edu/~nes/>. The mission of the National Election Studies (NES) is to "produce high quality data on voting, public opinion, and political participation that serve the research needs of social scientists, teachers, students, and policy makers concerned with understanding the theoretical and empirical foundations of mass politics in a democratic society."

Finally, several on-line sites allow curious individuals to conduct their own unscientific polls. See *Survey Central* at <http://www.apocalypse.org/~bill/survey>, *The Internet Voice* (the site where your opinion counts or at least we count your opinion) at <http://www.virtua.com/voice/>, and *Open Debate* at <http://www.opendebate.com/>. The poll creator follows the instructions at these sites and poses a question to fellow net users, the site itself then takes care of tabulating the results.

Using Your Knowledge

1. Locate the *Gallup Poll* volumes in the reference section of your library. Find the polls taken on the issue of abortion in 1969, 1972, 1974, 1981, 1983, 1992, and 1996. Make a graph showing the opinion distribution of the sample as a whole for each poll you find. Are the opinion distributions you find skewed, normal, or bimodal? Next, make a line graph showing the percentage selecting "favor" in each of these polls. Is the opinion distribution stable or unstable over time?

2. Using the data you gathered in Exercise 1, look at the opinions of the subgroups identified (religion, age, region, or whatever), and compare these opinions to the average opinion for the sample as a whole. Is opinion in any of the subgroups particularly skewed? Does opinion in any of the subgroups shift over time?

3. Starting with the September, 1997 poll, use the on-line version of the Gallup Poll to track public opinion on possible Democratic and Republican presidential candidates in the 2000 election.

4. Visit one of the Internet polling sites mentioned in the Research and Resources section and try conducting your own poll on a political issue of interest to you. Report the results and include in your report a discussion of why your poll would be considered "unscientific." What factors serve to limit confidence in the accuracy of this type of on-line poll?

Sample Exam Questions

Multiple-Choice Questions

1. A review of American attitudes toward capital punishment shows that
   a. public attitudes toward government policies remain stable over time.
   b. citizens will not register opinions on matters outside their expertise.
   c. public opinion places boundaries on allowable types of public policy.
   d. the government never does what the people want.

2. Opinion polling
   a. is a modern invention.
   b. dates back to colonial times.
   c. is the main method of ensuring that bills passed by the legislature always reflect the will of the people.
   d. is more useful to the pluralist than the majoritarian concept of politics.

3. Which of the following is *not* a way of describing the shape of a distribution of public opinion on an issue?
   a. Normal
   b. Stable
   c. Bimodal
   d. Skewed

4. Political conflict is more likely when public opinion is
   a. distributed normally.
   b. skewed toward the liberal side.
   c. skewed toward the conservative side.
   d. distributed bimodally.

5. Most people link their earliest recollections of politics with
   a. their family.
   b. their school experience.
   c. youth groups.
   d. their community.

6. The collective attitude of the citizens on a given issue or question is called
   a. public opinion.
   b. political knowledge.
   c. political ideology.
   d. political socialization.

7. The more educated people are,
   a. the more likely they are to favor redistribution of income.
   b. the more likely they are to think abortion should be a matter of a woman's choice.
   c. the less likely they are to value freedom over order.
   d. the less tolerant they are of dissent.

8. Which of the following is *most* likely to favor government action to limit abortion?
   a. A Catholic
   b. A person who views the Bible as God's actual word
   c. A person who views the Bible as inspired by God, but not literally true
   d. A person who views the Bible as a book of stories produced by humans

9. For students, saying the pledge of allegiance, attending Boys' or Girls' State, and participating in college-level mock elections are all exercises in
   a. public opinion.
   b. political knowledge.
   c. political ideology.
   d. political socialization.

10. The general term for voters who view the scope and purpose of government in terms of a consistent set of values and beliefs is
    a. *ideologue.*
    b. *liberal.*
    c. *conservative.*
    d. *capitalist.*

11. In America, communitarians tend to be prominent
    a. among people with low education and income.
    b. among people with high education and income.
    c. in the West.
    d. in the Northeast.

12. Which of the following is suggested by the analysis of ideological tendencies in the 1996 opinion sample?
    a. Conservatives are most common, but the four types are nearly equal.
    b. Most Americans are conservative ideologues.
    c. Liberals vastly outnumber conservatives.
    d. Libertarians are most common, but the four types are nearly equal.

13. The poll was notably wrong in the presidential election of
    a. 2000.
    b. 1948.
    c. 1992.
    d. 1996.

14. The case of the INF treaty shows that
    a. leaders have no effect on public opinion.
    b. support for the proposal was based more on general faith in the president than on belief in his proposal.
    c. public opinion was able to silence INF opposition.
    d. Republicans are more likely to take cues from leaders than are Democrats.

15. The packets of preexisting beliefs that people apply to specific issues are called
    a. ideologies.
    b. opinion schemes.
    c. opinion distributions.
    d. opinion shapes.

16. If given the range of choices below, most Americans would probably classify themselves as
    a. liberal.
    b. moderate.
    c. conservative.
    d. libertarian.

17. Which of the following influences the accuracy of a sample?
    a. The way the sample is selected
    b. The amount of variation in the population
    c. The size of the sample
    d. All of the above

18. In their recent study of political knowledge, Delli Carpini and Keeter found the strongest single predictor of political knowledge to be
    a. ideology.
    b. income.
    c. education.
    d. region.

19. Viewed over time, public opinion on race relations is an example of
    a. people favoring order over equality.
    b. people favoring freedom over equality.
    c. a massive shift in public opinion.
    d. majoritarian democracy in action.

— 20. According to the Gallup Poll, one's likelihood to view Russia in a favorable light decreases dramatically with
    a. age.
    b. income.
    c. education.
    d. knowledge.

21. When different questions on the same issue produce similar distributions of opinion, the opinion distribution is said to be
    a. skewed.
    b. bimodal.
    c. stable.
    d. normal.

22. The makeup of a community influences how its political opinions are formed. For example, in a homogeneous community, there may be strong pressure for
    a. conformity to the dominant attitudes of the group.
    b. equal rights for gays and lesbians.
    c. programs (such as sex education) that run counter to community values.
    d. rejection of the individual's peer group.

23. The higher one's income,
    a. the less likely one is to choose policies emphasizing freedom.
    b. the less likely one is to believe that abortion should be a woman's choice.
    c. the more interested one is likely to be in promoting order and equality.
    d. the more likely one is to oppose government employment guarantees.

24. On which of the following types of issues is a "gender gap" likely to be found?
    a. Issues where freedom and order are in conflict
    b. Issues where women's rights are at stake, such as the abortion issue
    c. Issues involving government spending to promote equality
    d. All of the above

25. A Gallup Poll taken in 1997 show that only 69 percent of the American public could identify
    a. Speaker Hastert.
    b. Vice President Al Gore.
    c. President Clinton.
    d. Governor George Bush.

Essay Questions

1. What characteristics of American public opinion are revealed by examining public opinion on capital punishment?

2. What are the reasons for the low level of knowledge about politics among the American public?

3. How are race and religion related to political values?

4. Identify the three key agents of early political socialization. Describe ways in which they are influential.

5. Discuss the limitations of the one-dimensional, liberal-conservative typology of political ideology. How does the liberal-conservative typology compare to the fourfold classification developed in Chapters 1 and 5?

CHAPTER 6
The Mass Media

Learning Objectives

After reading this chapter you should be able to

- Define the key terms at the end of the chapter.
- Outline the technological changes and events that have influenced the development of the mass media in America.
- Explain who owns the media in America and how they are regulated by the government.
- Discuss the consequences of private ownership of the media.
- Assess the validity of charges of media bias.
- Explain how people acquire news through the media.
- Describe how the mass media contribute to political socialization.
- Indicate the ways in which the mass media influence political behavior.
- Evaluate the contribution the media make to democratic government.

The Mass Media and the Challenge of Democracy

The text's opening vignette illustrates the complexity of regulating press and speech because of the rise of the Internet, which crosses boundaries of a sovereign state.

The mass media link the people and the government by making possible a two-way flow of information. The media report government actions to the people, and they also poll the public to assess people's opinion on specific issues. Although both of these functions are critically important to the majoritarian model of democracy, pluralist democracy relies on more specialized channels of communication.

For a pluralist system to be democratic, however, open channels of access are necessary. Although the government originally regulated the airwaves simply to provide order, later government limitations on the freedom of broadcasters have helped provide greater equality of access to the airwaves. These limits include the equal opportunities rule, the reasonable access rule, and the fairness doctrine. Through these provisions, the government has required the electronic media to present opposing points of view. With the repeal of the fairness doctrine in 1987, the media became more of a free market. Furthermore, the Telecommunications Act of 1996 relaxed many restrictions on media ownership, thus allowing for greater concentration of the media in a limited number of hands. In 1999, the FCC voted to allow a single company to own two television stations in the same major market. This promotes freedom, but it limits equality. On the other hand, in terms of coverage of events over the years, the media have tended to promote social equality. This may be seen in coverage of the civil rights and women's movements.

The freedom issue of greatest interest to the media, not surprisingly, has been the question of freedom of expression. Yet, as this chapter indicates, media coverage of events can contribute to disorder. To accept any one value as absolute means paying a high price, and that is clearly the case with freedom of the press.

Chapter Overview

People, Government, and Communications

The media include the technical devices and processes used in mass communication, which allow individuals or groups to transmit information to large, heterogeneous, widely dispersed audiences. In democratic governments, the mass media promote a two-way flow of communication between citizens and the government. Today, media used in political communication include print media, such as newspapers and magazines; broadcast media, such as television and radio; and new forms of mass media, such as fax transmissions and the Internet.

Development of Mass Media in the United States

This chapter focuses on the political uses of mass media in the news industry (that is, print and broadcast journalism).

American newspapers offer broad, general coverage of contemporary topics. In the United States, newspapers generally began as party organs, sponsored by political parties to advocate their views. Large-circulation, independently owned daily newspapers grew up as new technologies made nationwide news gathering possible. The competition between newspapers that was characteristic of the nineteenth and early twentieth centuries had died out by the 1950s. By 1997, only 58 cities had more than one daily paper under separate ownership.

Magazines offer more specialized coverage of topics and often serve as forums for opinions rather than objective news reports. Even a magazine with a limited readership can exert influence by reaching attentive policy elites who in turn influence mass opinion.

Radio developed in the twenties and thirties and eventually became a truly national medium, linking stations across the country into a limited number of national networks. News personalities became nationally known.

Television technology spread after World War II, and today it reaches nearly every home in the nation. Stations are linked via several major networks. As television has evolved, the importance of newscasters has grown, as has the emphasis on exploiting the visual impact of news events.

Modern Forms of Group Media

The last quarter century witnessed the introduction of new technologies that have been used for political communications between groups with common interests. These include fax machines and the Internet. Fax machines enable campaign managers to communicate with their workers and allow interest-group members to send messages to their representatives. The Internet makes information readily available and even helps to break news. It also allows users to share their opinions.

Private Ownership of the Media

In America, both the print and electronic media are privately owned. While this gives the news industry great political freedom, it also means that news is selected for its mass audience appeal, as judged by its impact on readers or listeners, sensationalism, treatment of familiar people or life situations, close-to-home character, or timeliness. The mass media are part of the entertainment industry, and news, too, is part of the entertainment package. The new and controversial trend toward "infotainment," a mixture of journalism and theater, has further blurred the distinction between news and entertainment.

Ownership of the media in America has become more and more concentrated as the same corporations control many newspapers and radio and television stations.

Government Regulation of the Media

The broadcast media operate under the regulations of an independent regulatory commission, the Federal Communications Commission (FCC). The FCC licenses broadcasters using the airwaves. In 1996, in a bipartisan effort, Congress undertook a major overhaul of the framework created under the 1934 law that established the FCC. Limits on media ownership were relaxed, and rate regulations were lifted. One immediate effect of this new system was increased concentration of the media. The long-term effects of this complicated law—part of which was declared unconstitutional in 1998—are uncertain.

The First Amendment guarantee of freedom of the press has been taken to cover all the media and has helped make the U.S. news media among the freest in the world. Historically, the broadcast media, which use the public airwaves, have been subject to some government regulation such as the equal opportunities and reasonable access rules.

Reporting and Following the News

The news media serve five specific functions for the political system: (1) reporting the news, (2) interpreting the news, (3) influencing citizens' opinions, (4) setting the agenda for government action, and (5) socializing citizens about politics. They attempt to provide firsthand coverage of national news events. Their reporters may rely on news releases, news briefings, press conferences, leaks, and cultivation of background sources for their material. The tendency for news reporters to be grouped together in press rooms and to rely on the same sources of information has given rise to a style of reporting sometimes referred to as pack journalism.

Americans are more interested in domestic news, and their primary concern is being informed about their local community. In an effort to make news understandable and interesting to viewers, television typically concentrates its attention on individuals rather than on political institutions and on political horse races rather than campaign issues.

Since the 1960s, people have reported that they get more of their news from television than from any other source. However, studies have suggested that people's reliance on television for their news and their trust in the medium might be overstated. Furthermore, research also indicates that "the television hypothesis"—that TV is to blame for Americans' low level of political knowledge—oversimplifies the reality. They note that what people learn from different media is related to their cognitive skills. In addition, attentiveness to news tends to be related to people's level of education, age, and gender.

Political Effects of the Media

The mass media influence public opinion, the political agenda, and political socialization. People believe that the media influence public opinion, and some studies have shown systematic and dramatic opinion changes linked to television news coverage, particularly to policy positions taken by news commentators.

Nevertheless, most scholars believe that the real power of the media consists of its ability to set the national agenda. Through the kind of stories they cover, the media help define the issues that get government attention.

The media also act as agents of political socialization. In this regard, their role is often contradictory. On the one hand, they contribute to American self-confidence by supporting public celebrations as great media events; on the other hand, they give air time to events and activities that reduce the sense of national well-being. The entertainment divisions may promote the values of law-abiding citizens, or they may do the reverse. Some scholars maintain that the most important effect of the media is to further the dominance of the existing order; yet protests, strikes, and violence all receive extensive coverage.

Evaluating the Media in Government

Media executives function as gatekeepers, deciding which stories to report and how to handle them. Any selection process reflects something about the values of the selector, and in the case of the media, the process often leads to charges of media bias. News reporters have been criticized for liberal bias, while media owners are often charged with having a conservative bias. A study based on newspaper stories during the last weeks of the 2000 presidential election campaign showed that both major party candidates received negative coverage.

In general, the media improve the quality of information citizens receive about the government. They report public opinion. These functions help make responsible government possible.

The media have mobilized government action to advance racial and sexual equality. They also uphold the value of freedom, when the freedom in question is freedom of the press. Yet, press freedom may conflict with order and thus, like all democratic values, is not without its costs to society.

Key Terms

mass media	infotainment	horse race journalism
group media	political agenda	media event
attentive policy elites	equal opportunities rule	television hypothesis
two-step flow of communication	reasonable access rule	Federal Communication Commission (FCC)
newsworthiness	gatekeepers	

Research and Resources

Are you ready to become part of the attentive public? Why not get to know the public affairs magazines that help shape American opinion? The *Reader's Guide to Periodical Literature* and some of the other indexes briefly mentioned in Chapter 2 of this study guide will point you to articles in these publications. Many of them have set up Web sites where you can sample what they have to offer.

When you use publications for information, you should be aware that magazines often have an explicit or implicit ideological orientation. Certain publications present views from the American left; others give the opinions of those on the right. If you are trying to examine an issue thoroughly, you will probably want to weigh arguments from each side so it is important to make sure that not all of your background material comes from right-wing or left-wing publications.

Some important journals of opinion include the following.

- On the right:

    National Review. William F. Buckley's magazine, a long-time standard-bearer of conservative ideas. <http:www.townhall.com/nationalreview/>.

    The American Spectator. Often has a highly polemical tone. <http:www.spectator.org>.

    The Weekly Standard. A conservative publication that debuted in 1995.

- Somewhere in the center, generally striving for editorial balance:

    The Atlantic Monthly. A monthly publication that includes several lengthy articles each month on aspects of American foreign or domestic policy. <http://www.TheAtlantic.com/>.

Daedalus. An academic quarterly; each volume focuses on a single topic and offers a variety of viewpoints.

Harper's. Similar to *Atlantic*, it now includes readings excerpted from other works and a wonderful index of offbeat facts in the front of each issue. The index is among the features included in the on-line site. <http://www.harpers.org/>.

- On the left:

   The New Republic. A leading liberal periodical that has moved more to the right in recent years; highly opinionated and often acerbic. < http://www.thenewrepublic.com/>.

   The Nation. The oldest continuously published journal of opinion in the country; it covers wide-ranging political topics. <http://www.TheNation.com/>.

   The Progressive. Another venerable and respected journal of liberal thought. <http://www.progressive.org/>.

- And finally, some on-line addresses for "alternative" publications mentioned in the text:

   Mother Jones. <http://www.mojones.com/>.

   The Utne Reader. <http://www.utne.com/reader/magazine.html>.

- If you are unsure about a particular magazine's ideological leanings, here is one source you might consult:

   Katz, William A., and Linda Steinberg Katz. *Magazines for Libraries*, 9th ed. New York: Bowker, 1997.

Using Your Knowledge

1. Select one of the following controversial subjects:

   - welfare reform
   - affirmative action
   - abortion
   - reforming the income tax

   Using the *Reader's Guide to Periodical Literature* or another index and the Internet resources listed above, locate three or four articles on your topic in various magazines that have different ideological slants. Skim the articles. Do the opinions expressed in the articles seem to be consistent with the ideological orientations of the publications as described in the list above?

2. If it is possible in your television viewing area, watch two or three different evening network newscasts. Compare the stories covered in each. Make a log listing the stories in order, and record the length of each story. Compare the way each network treats each story. Do they use film footage? Is it relevant? Do they use graphics? Is the presentation strictly factual, or does a commentator give more of an editorial perspective?

3. Watch a television news broadcast, and select the major political story covered. Compare the television coverage of that event or issue with newspaper accounts of the same story. What are the differences and similarities in the two accounts?

4. Many television news services have establish on-line links which may be found at the end of the chapter in your textbook. Watch the television news program, and then check out the on-line service. For example, try the all-news station MSNBC and then visit their Web site at <http://www.msnbc.com>. How does using the Web site affect your political knowledge?

5. What is the difference between "conventional" and "unconventional" media? Compare the treatment of a major political news story on *A Current Affair* (on-line at <http://www.current-affair.com/>) or *Hard Copy*, or *Larry King Live* (on-line at <http://cnn.com/CNN/Programs/LarryKing/index.html>) with coverage of the same issue on the *PBS NewsHour with Jim Lehrer* (on-line at <http://www1.pbs. org/newshour/>) or the Sunday morning news programs such as *Meet the Press* (on-line at <www. msnbc.com/news/meetpress_front.org>), *This Week* (on-line at <http://abcnews.com/onair/thisweek/ index.html>), or *Face the Nation* (on-line at <http://www.cbs.com/navbar/news.html>).

Getting Involved

Students who want to learn more about the media from the inside may be interested in applying for internships with broadcasters, newspapers, magazines, or other media-related organizations. Here are a few of the opportunities available. Some may require previous experience in journalism, such as work on your college newspaper.

C-SPAN has internships for students interested in communications and politics. Students must meet three basic criteria: they must be a college junior or senior, they must be interning for college credit, and they must be able to work a minimum of sixteen hours per week. Address: C-SPAN, Internship Program, 400 N. Capitol Street, NW, Suite 650, Washington, DC 20001. Telephone: 202-737-3220.

The Center for Investigative Reporting, a nonprofit, independent organization committed to investigative reporting, offers six-month paid internships to students who want to pair off with senior reporters and learn the techniques of investigative journalism. For winter internships, the deadline is December 1; for summer, it is May 1. Address: The Center for Investigative Reporting, c/o Communications Director, 500 Howard Street, Suite 206, San Francisco, CA 94105. E-mail: CIR@igc.apc.org.

The *Los Angeles Times* hires interns for its California offices as well as one intern for its Washington bureau. Summer internships are eleven weeks long, with a December 1 application deadline; part-time internships lasting seventeen weeks are available in the fall and spring, with June 1 and October 1 deadlines, respectively. Address: The *Los Angeles Times*, Editorial Internships, Times Mirror Square, Los Angeles, CA 90053. Find them on-line at <http://www.latimes.com/>.

The *Philadelphia Inquirer* offers paid summer internships in reporting. Internships run from Memorial Day to late August. Applications are due in mid-January. For further information, contact: Internship Coordinator, 400 North Broad Street, P.O. Box 8263, Philadelphia, PA 19101. Find them on-line at <http://www2. phillynews.com/>.

The *Boston Globe* offers full-time paid work for summer interns from June 1 to Labor Day. The program also includes seminars on legal issues, constitutional issues, and other issues related to journalism. An application form must be obtained from the *Globe* and returned by the application deadline of November 15. For further information, contact: The *Boston Globe*, P.O. Box 2378, Boston MA 02107-2378. Telephone: (617) 929-2000. Find them on-line at <http://www.boston.com/globe/gloabout.htm>.

The *Washington Post* offers summer internships to current college juniors and seniors interested in journalism. For further information, contact: News Personnel, 5th Floor, The *Washington Post*, 1150 15th Street, NW, Washington, DC 20071. Telephone: (202) 334-6000. Visit their Web site at <http://www.washingtonpost.com/>.

The *NewsHour with Jim Lehrer* provides unpaid internships running twelve to sixteen weeks in New York, Washington, and Denver. For summer internships, apply by March 31; for fall, apply by July 31; and for spring, apply by October 31. For more information, write to PBS *NewsHour*, Internship Coordinator, 356 West Street, New York, NY 10019. Find them on-line at <http://www1.pbs.org/newshour/home.html>.

The *New Republic* offers paid internships to prospective journalists who wish to read unsolicited manuscripts, check facts, and write short articles, reviews, and editorials. The deadline for summer is February 1; for the academic year, May 1. Telephone: (202) 331-7494.

For a directory of political debates, check www.politics1.com.

Sample Exam Questions

Multiple-Choice Questions

1. A democracy is *best* served by the media when they
   a. allow for a two-way flow of information.
   b. allow for a one-way flow of information.
   c. emphasize the entertainment value of news.
   d. do not attempt to reflect popular views.

2. The first American newspapers
   a. were primarily intended to advertise products.
   b. featured nationwide news services.
   c. were mainly political organs.
   d. mainly featured comics, sensational journalism, photographs, and sports sections.

3. The fax machine and the Internet are examples of technologies *best* categorized as part of the
   a. mass media.
   b. group media.
   c. broadcast media.
   d. print media.

4. Ownership concentration in the media
   a. has been increasing.
   b. is tightly limited by the FCC under the 1996 Telecommunications Act.
   c. occurs only within specific media industries.
   d. has been avoided in the United States through private ownership of the media.

5. The mixing of news and theater to re-create or simulate an event is known as
   a. pack journalism.
   b. infotainment.
   c. horse race journalism.
   d. yellow journalism.

6. The broadcast media first came under regulation
   a. as part of Franklin D. Roosevelt's attempt to impose socialism.
   b. as a response to broadcasters' need for order on the airwaves.
   c. as an attempt to limit media concentration.
   d. to ensure political candidates equal treatment under the fairness doctrine.

7. Which of the following is *not* a consequence of private ownership of the broadcast media?
   a. Media dependence on advertising
   b. Media attention to ratings
   c. Media selection of stories based primarily on political significance
   d. Media emphasis on entertainment value in the presentation of news

8. Most Americans rely on which of the following as their *chief* news source?
   a. Newspapers
   b. Magazines
   c. Radio
   d. Television

9. Americans are *most* concerned about what is happening
   a. in the world.
   b. in their own community.
   c. to the President.
   d. in Congress.

10. When a person gives information which reporters may quote providing that they do not identify their source, the informant is said to be
    a. speaking "on background."
    b. "floating a trial balloon."
    c. speaking "off the record."
    d. none of the above.

11. Which of the following FCC regulation has been imposed on the print media?
    a. Equal opportunities rule
    b. Reasonable access rule
    c. Fairness doctrine
    d. None of the above

12. Television today promotes popular support for government through
    a. programs like *The X-files* and *NYPD Blue*.
    b. coverage of terrorism, assassinations, and protests.
    c. coverage of celebrations of national holidays.
    d. horse race journalism.

13. Magazines with limited circulations may still influence mass opinion
    a. indirectly through a two-step flow of communication.
    b. by appealing to a mass audience over the heads of the attentive policy elites.
    c. directly by increasing their number of subscribers.
    d. by appealing to a majoritarian rather than a pluralist concept of democracy.

14. Most news about Congress comes from
    a. reporters' accounts of floor debates.
    b. C-SPAN broadcasts.
    c. congressional press releases.
    d. the speaker of the house and the majority leader of the Senate.

15. The tendency for journalists to adopt similar viewpoints toward the news because they associate with each other is known as
    a. gatekeeping.
    b. a feeding frenzy.
    c. pack journalism.
    d. yellow journalism.

16. Mass media are
    a. more important in the pluralist than in the majoritarian model of democracy.
    b. more important in the majoritarian than in the pluralist model of democracy.
    c. equally important to each model.
    d. unimportant in totalitarian states.

17. The mass media's coverage of the civil rights movement tended to advance
    a. equality.
    b. order.
    c. freedom.
    d. pluralism.

18. When media executives select events to report, they act as
    a. pack journalists.
    b. gatekeepers.
    c. checkbook journalists.
    d. infotainers.

19. The value *most* likely to be held as absolute by the media is
    a. freedom of expression.
    b. equality of access.
    c. social order.
    d. liberalism.

20. The FCC's equal opportunities rule requires that
    a. a station that sells time to one candidate must sell it to other candidates under the same conditions.
    b. stations must hire women and minorities in news anchor positions.
    c. stations must carry news of interest to each ethnic group in the community.
    d. minorities should receive additional opportunities to purchase television licenses.

21. The rule that obligated broadcasters to provide fair coverage of all views on public issues was
    a. called the fairness doctrine.
    b. introduced in 1987.
    c. known as the equal access rule.
    d. declared unconstitutional by the Supreme Court.

22. Compared with the British and Germans, American television reporters
    a. are less likely to present candidates' activities in a neutral fashion.
    b. are less likely to make reinforcing comments about a candidate's activities.
    c. are less likely to make deflating comments about a candidate's activities.
    d. are none of the above.

23. In judging the newsworthiness of a story, the primary criterion used is
    a. political significance.
    b. audience appeal.
    c. educational value.
    d. broad social importance.

24. The likelihood of a newspaper making an endorsement in the 2000 presidential election was closely linked to
    a. the size of the newspaper's circulation.
    b. the size of the city.
    c. the number of partisans in the city.
    d. none of the above.

25. The reasonable access rule requires broadcasters to
    a. make their stations accessible to wheelchair users.
    b. discuss public issues and provide fair coverage to each side of an issue.
    c. make equal time available on the same terms to all candidates for an office.
    d. make their facilities available for the expression of conflicting views by responsible elements of the community.

Essay Questions

1. Explain the complexity of regulating freedom of press and speech in the world of the Internet.

2. Explain how media executives, news editors, and reporters function as gatekeepers in directing news flow. What types of news are likely to get through the gate?

3. Are the national news media biased? Answer this question by discussing research outlined in the chapter.

4. What are the consequences of private ownership of the media? Explain how concentration of media ownership might undermine democratic government.

5. Discuss the strengths and limitations of media influence on political behavior.

CHAPTER 7
Participation and Voting

Learning Objectives

After reading this chapter you should be able to

- Define the key terms at the end of the chapter.
- Distinguish between conventional and unconventional participation.
- Explain the difference between particularized participation and activities that are geared to influence broad policy.
- Compare American political participation with participation in other democracies.
- Discuss the extension of suffrage to African Americans, women, and eighteen-year-olds.
- Explain the nature of initiatives, referendums, and recalls.
- Account for the low voter turnout in the United States.
- Evaluate the extent to which various forms of political participation enhance freedom, order, or equality.
- Assess the extent to which the various forms of participation fit the pluralist or majoritarian models of democracy.

Participation and Voting and the Challenge of Democracy

Free participation in democracy means citizens must be allowed to choose whether or not to participate. It also means they may use the resources at their disposal to try to influence the government. Freedom thus favors those who have the most resources to advance their interests.

Equal participation means every citizen's ability to influence government should be equal to every other citizen's, so that a lack of personal sources does not work to the disadvantage of anyone.

At one time in the United States, safeguarding order meant restricting participation. It meant not letting certain groups (women and African Americans) vote, for fear of upsetting the social order. Today, protecting order may mean opening up the political process so that groups have less incentive to engage in unconventional participation.

The most obvious function of elections is to allow citizens to choose among candidates or issues. In addition, elections also socialize political activity, institutionalize mass influence in politics, regularize access to power, and bolster the state's power and authority.

The majoritarian model assumes that government responds to popular wishes articulated through conventional channels, primarily voting in elections. The majoritarians count each vote equally and hence are biased toward the value of equality in participation. By emphasizing conventional participation, majoritarians come to resemble populists.

The pluralist model emphasizes freedom. Citizens are free to use all their resources to influence government at any of the many access points available to them. Thus, organizations, such as militia groups, have made extensive use of group media. Pluralism may seem to favor those with resources, but in contrast to majoritarianism, it allows plenty of room for unconventional political participation. Yet, when people are forced to rely on unconventional participation to be heard, it is hard to call the system democratic.

Chapter Overview

Democracy and Political Participation

Voting is central to democracy, but when voting is the only form of participation available, there is no real democracy. In addition to casting votes, citizens must also be able to discuss politics, form interest groups, contact public officials, campaign for competing parties, run for office, or protest government decisions, etc.

Political participation—the actions of private citizens that are intended to influence or support government or politics—may be either conventional or unconventional.

Unconventional Participation

Unconventional participation is relatively uncommon behavior that challenges the government and is personally stressful to participants and their opponents. Unconventional acts might include protest demonstrations, boycotts, blocking traffic, and so forth. In recent years, an international form for unconventional participation involving citizens of many countries has developed.

Support for Unconventional Participation

Despite a tradition dating back to the Boston Tea Party, unconventional participation is frowned on by most Americans, especially when it disrupts their daily lives. Yet, Americans are more likely to engage in unconventional political participation than are citizens of other democratic states. Researchers find unconventional participation hard to study but suggest that groups resort to unconventional participation precisely because they are powerless and have been denied access to conventional channels of participation. Despite the public's belief that unconventional participation is generally ineffective, direct political action sometimes works. Unconventional actions such as protests and marches tend to appeal to those who distrust the political system, have a strong sense of political efficacy, and manage to develop a sense of group consciousness.

Conventional Participation

The comparatively high rate of unconventional political participation presents a dilemma for American democracy, since the whole point of democratic politics is to make political participation conventional. Conventional political behavior includes (1) actions that show support for government, such as participation in patriotic celebrations and (2) actions that try to change or influence government policies, either to secure personal benefits or to achieve broad policy objectives.

Attempts to achieve broad policy objectives include activities that require little initiative (voting) and those that require high initiative (attending meetings, persuading others to vote in a certain way, attending congressional hearings, running for office). People also participate by using the court system (for example, by joining in class-action suits). Americans are less likely to vote than citizens in other democracies, but they are more likely to participate in other conventional ways.

Participation Through Voting

In America, the right to vote was extended only gradually to various groups (African Americans, women, eighteen-year-olds). For much of America's history, the nation departed considerably from the democratic ideal; yet, in comparison with other countries, the United States has a good record of providing for equality in voting rights.

In addition to selecting candidates for office, citizens of some states vote on issues by means of referenda and initiatives, two devices not available on the national level. In 2000, voters in 42 states approved 204 initiatives or referenda. These help representative democracy more closely resemble direct democracy, but they are not without drawbacks. For one thing, they are quite expensive; for another, referendum campaigns often increase rather than decrease the impact of special-interest groups. Some twenty states also provide for recalls, or special elections to remove an officeholder.

Voting for candidates is the most visible form of political participation. It serves democratic government by allowing citizens to choose the candidates they think would make the best public officials and then to hold officials accountable for their actions in government, either by re-electing or removing them. This assumes citizens are knowledgeable about what officials do and participate actively by going to the polls.

America holds more elections and has more offices subject to election than do other countries. However, American participation in elections is very low compared with that of other democracies.

Explaining Political Participation

Not only is voter turnout in the United States comparatively low, it has also declined over time. However, other forms of participation are high and are on the increase.

Conventional participation is often related to socioeconomic status. The higher a person's education, income, or occupational status, the more likely he or she is to vote or use other conventional means to influence government. On the other hand, unconventional participation is less clearly related to socioeconomic status. Over the years, race, sex, and marital status have been related to participation in the United States. But the single most influential factor affecting conventional participation is education.

Arguments now advanced to explain the decline in voter turnout point to the influx of new, young voters enfranchised under the Twenty-Sixth Amendment. Young voters are less likely to vote. Other reasons offered include the growing belief that the government is unresponsive to citizens and the decline in people's identification with a political party. In addition, American political parties are not as closely linked to specific groups as are parties in other democracies; such links between parties and groups often help to mobilize voters.

Another possible explanation for the low U.S. turnout is that it is more difficult to vote here than in other countries. In the United States, citizens are required to register in advance, which leaves the initiative up to the individual citizen. Registration requirements work to reduce the number of people actually eligible to vote on election day. The "motor voter" law makes it easier to register and is expected to increase participation. A final explanation for low turnout is that although the act of voting is relatively simple, learning about candidates takes a great deal of initiative, and many eligible voter may feel inadequate to the task.

Participation and Freedom, Equality, and Order

Whereas the relationships between participation and freedom and between participation and equality are clear, the relationship between participation and order is more complicated. Groups that resort to unconventional participation may threaten the social order and even the government itself. The passage of the Twenty-Sixth Amendment, which lowered the voting age to eighteen, is an example of a government effort to try to channel unconventional participation (strikes and protests) into conventional participation (voting) and thereby maintain order.

Participation and Models of Democracy

In addition to their role in selecting officeholders, elections also serve to (1) socialize political activity, (2) institutionalize access to political power, and (3) bolster the state's power and authority. Majoritarian participation focuses on elections and emphasizes equality and order. The decentralized American system of government allows for many forms of participation in addition to voting in elections, and this type of pluralism emphasizes freedom of individuals and groups.

Key Terms

political participation	unconventional participation	supportive behavior
conventional participation	direct action	influencing behavior

class-action suit	progressivism	referendum
suffrage	direct primary	initiative
franchise	recall	standard socioeconomic model

Research and Resources

For people interested in political parties and elections, *Congressional Quarterly's Guide to U.S. Elections*, 3rd ed. (Washington, D.C.: Congressional Quarterly Press, 1994) offers a gold mine of information. Among other things, the volume includes popular vote tallies for the following:

- the U.S. House of Representatives from 1824–1992
- the U.S. Senate from 1913–1992 (remember, senators were elected by state legislatures before 1913)
- governorships from 1789–1992
- presidential primaries from 1912–1992
- southern primaries (a special focus since in the "solid South" the real political battle has occurred in the primary, not the general election).

Another good source of voting data is the *America Votes* series edited by Richard Scammon and Alice McGillivray (also published by Congressional Quarterly Press). This handbook provides county-by-county election returns for general elections for presidents, senators, representatives, and governors. It also gives election totals of primary contests for these offices.

Both of these works are great for providing actual election results. However, they do not help you much if you want to investigate some of the issues raised about how people evaluate candidates and how they participate in politics outside the voting booth. To find out more about these issues, you might turn to the bibliographies given at the end of Chapters 5, 7, or 9; but even if you read every book listed, you might not find the specific answer to the exact question that interests you. A useful source for biographies of candidates, campaign finances, issue positions by using the National Political Awareness Test, special interest groups, and voting records is www.vote-smart.org.

You may want to find out if computerized survey data are available on your campus. The authors of *The Challenge of Democracy* have put together a data set to complement this text. You may want to check with your instructor to see if these materials (called Crosstabs) are available for your use. Alternatively, your government or political science department may have acquired election surveys provided by the American Political Science Association as part of its SETUPS series. Each SETUPS comes with a student guide that shows how to manipulate data. Finally, if your college or university is a member of the Inter-university Consortium for Political and Social Research (ICPSR), it may tap into vast quantities of data from that source. Visit the ICPSR's Web site at <http://www.icpsr.umich.edu/>.

Using Your Knowledge

1. Using the *Guide to U.S. Elections*, find the election returns for your county for the last three presidential election years. Compare the returns in the presidential races with those in the contests for the House of Representatives. What differences do you notice? Next, compare the House votes in presidential years with those in the intervening, off years. How do the turnout totals compare?

2. Interview a person who has engaged in unconventional participation. Find out what form this unconventional participation took, what the participant's motivation was, and whether he or she felt the activity was successful. What led your interviewee to choose unconventional participation rather than conventional participation?

Getting Involved

Voting

The most basic way to participate in American politics is to vote, but as the chapter points out, in order to vote, you must first be registered. "Motor voter" legislation made the task easier by allowing people to register by simply mailing in a card; in addition, there are some Internet sites available that will help you obtain and fill out the forms needed for registration and also apply for an absentee ballot. The Democratic Party offers such a site at <http://democratic-party.org/voter/>. You can use this service even if you are not a Democrat, but if you prefer help from a nonpartisan source, try Rock the Vote at <http://www.rockthevote.org/>. Rock the Vote also offers opportunities for volunteers.

Students who study abroad can still vote. The Federal Voting Assistance Program, located within the Office of the Secretary of Defense, administers the Uniformed and Overseas Citizens Absentee Voting Act (UOCAVA) which requires that the states and territories allow U.S. citizens to register and vote absentee in elections for federal office. The FVAP also provides non-partisan voter information. Find them on the Web at <http://www.fvap.gov/>.

Internships

Project Vote Smart, a nonprofit, nonpartisan, grassroots effort, offers internships during the summer and throughout the school year. Interns cover every member of Congress, governors, and the president; they put out national surveys, compile performance evaluations and campaign finance information, work with journalists, and operate a database that supplies voter information. Contact the National Internship Coordinator, PVS National Internship Program, 129 NW 4th Street, Suite 204, Corvallis, OR 97330. Telephone: (541) 754-2746 or (541) 737-3760. E-mail: <intern@vote-smart.org> or <ann@vote-smart.org>. Extensive information on these internships is available on-line at <http://www.vote-smart.org/about/help/nip/nip.htm>.

Sample Exam Questions

Multiple-Choice Questions

1. In a democracy, elections are
   a. both necessary and sufficient to guarantee democratic government.
   b. necessary but not sufficient to guarantee democratic government.
   c. sufficient but not necessary to guarantee democratic government.
   d. neither necessary nor sufficient to guarantee democratic government.

2. Which of the following would *least* likely be considered conventional political participation in the United States?
   a. Persuading people to sign a petition
   b. Writing a letter to a public official
   c. Marching in a demonstration
   d. Training with a militia group

3. Which of the following *best* describes the effectiveness of unconventional participation?
   a. Unconventional participation is never effective.
   b. Unconventional participation is sometimes effective, but only if it is peaceful.
   c. Both violent and nonviolent unconventional participation are sometimes effective.
   d. Unconventional participation is the most effective means available to upper-level socioeconomic groups.

4. When citizens contact city officials in order to oppose the establishment of a nuclear waste facility in their area, they are
   a. engaged in conventional participation.
   b. giving an example of the "NIMBY" phenomenon.
   c. seeking a particular benefit.
   d. doing all of the above.

5. Direct political action appeals *most* to those who
   a. distrust the political system.
   b. have little sense of political efficacy.
   c. are unable to develop a strong sense of group consciousness.
   d. do all of the above.

6. The first step in extending full voting rights to African Americans came when
   a. Farrakhan led the Million Man March.
   b. the Supreme Court struck down a law preventing African Americans from voting in primaries.
   c. the Supreme Court ruled that state poll taxes were unconstitutional.
   d. Congress passed the Voting Rights Act.

7. Which of the following *best* describes American political participation in comparison with activities of citizens in other democracies?
   a. Americans are more likely to vote and participate in lower-initiative activities.
   b. Americans are more likely to participate in higher-initiative activities.
   c. Americans are less likely to participate in higher-initiative activities.
   d. Americans are less likely to participate in unconventional activities.

8. African American males were enfranchised by the
   a. Fourteenth Amendment.
   b. Fifteenth Amendment.
   c. Nineteenth Amendment.
   d. Twenty-Sixth Amendment.

9. The Nineteenth Amendment enfranchised
   a. African American females.
   b. African American males.
   c. eighteen-year-olds.
   d. none of the above.

10. When Californians voted to permit medical use of marijuana, they did so via
    a. unconventional participation.
    b. an initiative.
    c. a recall.
    d. a referendum.

11. Which of the following may be used at the level of the national government?
    a. A referendum
    b. An initiative
    c. A class-action suit
    d. All of the above

12. Which of the following could be said about African American southern voter registration in the South in 1996?
    a. The percentage of African American registered voters had more than doubled since 1960.
    b. The percentage of African American registered voters was largely unchanged following the passage of the 1965 Civil Rights Act.
    c. The percentage of African American registered voters continued to trail white registration substantially.
    d. None of the above.

13. Which of the following is *most* important in predicting conventional political participation in American politics?
    a. Education
    b. Race
    c. Sex
    d. Region

14. If voters are to hold public officials accountable through the electoral process, then which of the following assumptions must hold true?
    a. Officeholders must be motivated to respond to public opinion by the threat of defeat.
    b. Citizens must know the candidates and their actions in office.
    c. Citizens must participate activity in the electoral process.
    d. All of the above.

15. The decline in voter turnout since the 1960s has been associated with all of the following *except*
    a. lower levels of participation by women.
    b. lower levels of participation by young people.
    c. lower levels of party identification.
    d. the complexity of the registration process.

16. In the area of political participation, majoritarians would be *most* likely to value
    a. equality and order over freedom.
    b. freedom and equality over order.
    c. order and freedom over equality.
    d. equality and freedom over order.

17. In the area of political participation, pluralists emphasize
    a. freedom.
    b. equality.
    c. order.
    d. conventional participation only.

18. The standard socioeconomic model would predict that
    a. people with low incomes are most likely to vote.
    b. older people are more likely to vote.
    c. women are most likely to resort to unconventional participation.
    d. white-collar professionals are most likely to participate in politics.

19. The Boston Tea Party and the march from Selma to Montgomery are two examples of
    a. communist tactics.
    b. conventional participation.
    c. unconventional participation.
    d. institutionalized politics.

20. The passage of the Voting Rights Act of 1965
    a. gave women the right to vote.
    b. gave eighteen-year-olds the right to vote.
    c. put states under federal supervision to protect African American voting rights.
    d. led to the Selma march.

21. Protestors in Washington have succeeded in all of the following *except*
    a. disrupting the business in a significant part of downtown Washington.
    b. raising public awareness of IMF policies.
    c. preventing an IMF meeting.
    d. emboldening a new generation of activists in the United States and abroad.

22. When the Constitution was first approved, the right to vote was
    a. extended to all white people.
    b. essentially determined by state legislatures.
    c. extended to all property owners.
    d. specifically denied to African Americans, women, and those under twenty-one years of age.

23. Progressivism is associated with which of the following?
    a. Direct primaries
    b. Private primaries
    c. White primaries
    d. Integrated primaries

24. A key strategy Martin Luther King, Jr., used in the civil rights movement was
    a. organizing mass letter-writing campaigns to legislators.
    b. direct action to challenge specific cases of discrimination.
    c. holding legislators accountable at the ballot box.
    d. lobbying southern legislators.

25. By the 1997–1998 election cycle, over half of all voter registration took place through
    a. county offices.
    b. private offices.
    c. state offices.
    d. motor vehicle agencies.

Essay Questions

1. Citizen participation in elections is necessary for a modern representative democracy, but elections themselves are not enough to make a government democratic. Why? Explain the additional forms of political behavior assumed by the pluralist and majoritarian models of democracy.

2. Discuss the legacy of the Progressives with respect to political participation. What mechanisms did they promote to increase political participation? Have these measures produced better government? Why or why not?

3. Explain why people resort to unconventional political participation. Is it ever effective? Give examples to illustrate your answer.

4. Are Americans politically apathetic? In your answer, compare American political participation with the participation of citizens in other democracies.

5. Explain the reasons for international protest against institutions like the IMF and the World Bank.

CHAPTER 8
Political Parties

Learning Objectives

After reading this chapter you should be to

- Define the key terms at the end of the chapter.
- Describe the four most important functions of political parties.
- Trace the history of the major political parties in America.
- List the functions performed by minor parties.
- Account for the emergence of a two-party system in the United States.
- Assess the extent of party identification in the United States and its influence on voters' choices.
- Summarize the ideological and organizational differences between Republicans and Democrats.
- Decide whether the American system is more pluralist or majoritarian in its operation.

Political Parties and the Challenge of Democracy

On the face of it, the American two-party system seems tailor-made for majoritarian democracy. The parties structure the vote into two broad categories and reduce the opportunities for narrowly focused small groups to gain control of the government apparatus. The party system reduces the amount of information voters need to make rational choices. Yet, even this seemingly majoritarian device does not fully realize its majoritarian potential.

Majority parties are not always able to implement the policies they favor, for example. This is partly because they lack effective party discipline. That deficiency, in turn, is related to the decentralized structure of American parties. In a sense, America has, not two, but one hundred and two parties—two national organizations and two major parties in each of the fifty states.

On the whole, Democrats and Republicans do differ with respect to their political ideologies. The Democrats are more liberal and tend to place a high value on political and social equality. They are willing to use the government to achieve a more egalitarian economy and society, but they do not wish to use the government to restrict individual freedom (in matters related to lifestyles, reproductive choices, or freedom of expression, for example) to protect the social order. Republicans, on the other hand, are more likely to prefer order and freedom to equality; they prefer limited government when issues of equality are at stake, but they are often willing to use government power to support a particular vision of social order that restricts access to abortion, prohibits homosexual activity, and promotes prayer in public schools.

However, these general statements of ideological differences *between* the parties tend to obscure the fact that there are ideological differences *within* the parties as well. Nonetheless, the difficulties American parties have in maintaining discipline and coordinating the actions of government officials make it hard for them to fulfill the ideals of the majoritarian model. The 2000 presidential election proves that though the two parties dominate American politics, a third party can spoil a victory for one of the two major parties.

Chapter Overview

Political Parties and Their Functions

A political party is an organization that sponsors candidates for office under the organization's name. The link between political parties and democracy is so close that many democratic theorists believe democracy would be impossible in modern nation-states without parties. Parties perform several important functions in a political system, including the following:

1. *Nominating candidates for election to public office.* This provides a form of quality control through peer review by party insiders who know candidates well and judge their acceptability. Parties may also take an active role in recruiting talented candidates for office.

2. *Structuring voting choices.* Parties reduce the number of candidates on a ballot to those that have a realistic chance of winning. This reduces the amount of information voters must acquire to make rational decisions.

3. *Proposing alternative government programs.* Parties specify policies their candidates will pursue if elected. These proposed policies usually differ between the parties.

4. *Coordinating the actions of government officials.* Parties help bridge the separation of powers, to produce coordinated policies that are effective in governing the country.

A History of U.S. Party Politics

Today, political parties are institutionalized parts of the American political process. But they were not even mentioned in the Constitution. Although there were opposing factions from the beginning, the first party system only began to develop during the Washington administration, and the function of parties in nominating candidates did not emerge clearly until the election of 1800. In this early system, electoral contests between the two parties, the Federalists and the Democratic Republicans, revealed a flaw in constitutional design for choosing a president and vice president. The Twelfth Amendment, which provided for separate election of these two positions, tacitly recognized that future American elections would be contested by pairs of candidates who shared party affiliation. By 1820, the Democratic Republicans so dominated this system that the Federalists did not even field a candidate. Soon, factionalism developed within the Democratic Republican Party, and a new party system emerged.

The first system had developed during a period when suffrage was very limited and there was little popular participation in the electoral process. As states began to allow popular selection of presidential electors and also relax voting requirements, the outlines of the first popular national political parties began to emerge in Andrew Jackson's Democrats and John Quincy Adams's Whigs. Parties began to hold national conventions and draft party platforms. Slavery and sectionalism eventually destroyed the Whigs and led to the formation of a new party opposed to the spread of slavery, the Republican Party.

Thus, the election of 1856 marked the first contest between Democrats and Republicans, the parties constituting our present-day party system. Since then, there have been three critical elections signaling new, enduring electoral realignments in which one or the other of the two parties became dominant. In the period from 1860 to 1894, there was a rough balance between the parties. From the critical election of 1896 until 1930, a period of Republican dominance followed. The critical election of 1932 produced a Democratic majority, which persisted largely unbroken until 1994, when the Republicans gained control of both houses of Congress. We may currently be in a period of electoral dealignment, in which party loyalties are less important to voters.

The American Two-Party System

The history of American party politics has been dominated by successive two-party systems, but minor parties—including bolter parties, farm-labor parties, ideological protest parties, and single-issue parties—have made special contributions to American politics. Although third parties have not generally fared well as vote getters, they have helped people express discontent with the choices offered by the dominant parties. Third parties function as policy advocates and as safety valves for the system.

The persistence of the two-party system in America has been aided by the country's election rules. In U.S. elections, single winners are chosen by a simple plurality of votes. A presidential candidate wins election by amassing a majority of electoral votes. The federal structure itself also contributes to the staying power of the Democrats and Republicans. Even when one party wins a landslide presidential election, the loser is still likely to retain significant strength in many individual states. This makes it possible for the minority party to rebuild.

The longevity of the present two-party system is also a result of the tendency for citizens to be socialized from childhood to think of themselves as Democrats or Republicans. They identify with one or the other party, and this identification predisposes them to vote for candidates of that party. Whereas a citizen's actual voting behavior may change from election to election or from candidate to candidate, party identification changes more slowly over time, as citizens who find themselves voting against their party gradually reassess their identification.

Party Ideology and Organization

The Democratic and Republicans parties differ substantially on ideology. More Republicans than Democrats consider themselves as conservative. The 2000 platform of the Republicans called for tax cuts, more military spending, and smaller government. On the other hand, the Democratic platform advocated active but smaller government, fiscal discipline, free trade, and tough crime policies.

The federal structure is apparent in the organization of the country's political parties. Each party has separate state and national organizations. At the national level, each party has a national convention, national committee, congressional party conference, and congressional campaign committee. Historically, the role of the national organizations was fairly limited; but in the 1970s, Democratic procedural reforms and Republican organizational reforms increased the activity of the national organizations. The national organizations have increased in strength and financial resources, yet state party organizations are still essentially independent in organizing their state activities, and so the system remains decentralized.

The Model of Responsible Party Government

Responsible parties are a key feature of majoritarian theory. For a party system to work, the following four things are necessary: (1) the parties must present clear, coherent programs; (2) the voters must choose candidates on the basis of these programs; (3) the winning party must carry out its program; and (4) the voters must hold the incumbents responsible for their program at the next election. This chapter argues that the first and third criteria are met in American democracy. The next chapter looks more closely at the remaining features.

Key Terms

political party	critical election	party identification
nomination	electoral realignment	national committee
political system	two-party system	party conference
electoral college	electoral dealignment	congressional campaign committee
caucus	majority representation	party machine
national convention	proportional representation	responsible party government
party platform		

Research and Resources

This chapter indicates that the American system is built on a loose confederation of independent, state party organizations rather than a rigidly hierarchical structure with a national party at its apex. Indeed, until very recently, the national party all but went out of existence in nonpresidential election years. Thus, the two most conspicuous products of national party organizations have been the presidential nominating conventions and the party platforms.

If you are interested in doing research on party conventions or platforms, the following two reference works are especially useful.

Johnson, Donald Bruce. *National Party Platforms, 1840–1976.* 6th ed. Urbana: University of Illinois Press, 1978. Chronologically arranged compendium of party platforms. There is also a supplement, *National Party Platforms of 1980.*

National Party Conventions, 1831–1996. Washington, D.C.: Congressional Quarterly Press, 1997. This publication includes excerpts of party platforms, as well as chronologies of nominating conventions and state-by-state votes of delegates on issues placed before the conventions. In addition to this work, the Congressional Quarterly's *Guide to U.S. Elections*, mentioned in the last chapter, also provides a wealth of information on these topics.

A few party platforms are available on-line at <gopher://wiretap.spies.com:70/11/Gov/Platform>. Your text contains URLs for the Web sites of major and minor American political parties. For information about parties all over the world, try <http://www.luna.nl/~benne/politics/parties.html>. To get information on the two major political parties as well as about 40 minor parties, check www.politics1.com, which provides direct links to the various parties. The site www.selectsmart.com allows you to see which political party most closely resembles your views.

Using Your Knowledge

1. Visit the Democratic and Republican Web sites at <http://www.dnc.org> and <http://www.rnc.org>, respectively. What similarities and differences do you notice in the information and services available at each site?

2. Find and read the Democratic and Republican party platforms for an election held within the last twenty years. Note the areas of similarity and difference between the two. In the election year you chose to examine, would you say that observers who might have claimed "there's not a dime's worth of difference between the two parties" would have been correct? Give evidence to support your answer.

3. Using the Gallup Poll or other available survey data (see Chapter 5 of this guide), research changes in party identification over the last twenty years.

Getting Involved

If you are interested in working for a political party, you may want to begin by contacting the local party organization in your county or joining the Young Democrats or Young Republicans on your campus. The congressional campaign Web sites for the two parties provide some help for those who want to volunteer: Republicans at <http://www.rccc.org> and <http://www.rscc.org>, Democrats at <http://www.dccc.org> and <http://www.dscc.org>. There are some internships available for students who would like to become involved with the parties on the national level. For example, the Democratic Congressional Campaign Committee uses twenty-five to thirty unpaid interns to do research, assist in fund-raising, work with communications, and tend to mail and administrative details. If you are interested in learning more, contact them at Internship Coordinator, Democratic Congressional Campaign Committee, 430 South Capitol Street, Second Floor, Washington, D.C. 20003.

Sample Exam Questions

Multiple-Choice Questions

1. New Zealand and Great Britain are both examples of countries with
   a. absolute monarchs.
   b. proportional representation.
   c. two-party systems.
   d. a strong multiparty tradition.

2. One way that parties differ from interest groups is that parties
   a. contribute funds to candidates.
   b. sponsor candidates for office as their avowed representative.
   c. represent identifiable interests.
   d. mobilize get-out-the-vote campaigns.

3. Which of the following is *not* among the four most important functions of a political party?
   a. Nominating candidates for office
   b. Proposing alternative government policies
   c. Raising money for candidates
   d. Structuring the voting choice

4. A critical election is one in which
   a. an incumbent president is defeated.
   b. an electoral realignment occurs.
   c. divided government is produced.
   d. divided government is ended.

5. The development of the first party system uncovered problems in the method of electing the president and vice president. The Twelfth Amendment solved these problems by
   a. creating the electoral college.
   b. dissolving the electoral college.
   c. requiring separate votes for president and vice president.
   d. requiring presidential candidates to select their running mates.

6. The first election in which presidential electors in most states were chosen by popular vote was the election of
   a. 1816.
   b. 1820.
   c. 1824.
   d. 1828.

7. The second party system in the United States, which featured Democrats and Whigs, fell apart because of
   a. slavery and sectionalism.
   b. rum, Romanism, and rebellion.
   c. the electoral dominance of the Democratic Party.
   d. the personal magnetism of Abraham Lincoln.

8. Which of the following is *not* considered to have been a critical election?
   a. 1860
   b. 1896
   c. 1920
   d. 1932

9. The Democratic coalition under Franklin Roosevelt included all of the following *except*
   a. southern whites.
   b. northern Protestant businessmen.
   c. Jews.
   d. Catholics.

10. The Prohibition Party is an example of
    a. a bolter party.
    b. a single-issue party.
    c. a farmer-labor party.
    d. a party of ideological protest.

11. In the 1995–1996 election cycle, Republican national, senatorial, and congressional committees
    a. raised less money than did the Democrats.
    b. tightly controlled the campaigns of Republican candidates.
    c. received most of their contributions from unions.
    d. did none of the above.

12. Minor parties often contribute to the political process by
    a. transforming themselves into major parties.
    b. acting as safety valves, which allows their followers to express their discontent.
    c. getting enough votes to change electoral outcomes.
    d. getting enough votes to win election.

13. Which of the following contributes to the persistence of the two-party system?
    a. Constitutional recognition of two parties
    b. Proportional representation
    c. Political socialization
    d. All of the above

14. The 2000 Republican platform supported all of the following *except*
    a. tax cuts.
    b. more military spending.
    c. smaller government.
    d. abolishing the Department of Education.

15. Which of the following characterizes the American party system today?
    a. There are far fewer Independents than Democrats and Republicans combined.
    b. There are more Republicans than Democrats.
    c. The Democrats are increasing in comparison to Republicans and Independents.
    d. All of the above.

16. Which of the following is *not* a function of national party organizations in the United States?
    a. Holding quadrennial national conventions
    b. Maintaining congressional campaign committees
    c. Directing and controlling presidential campaigns
    d. Raising money to supplement funds raised by congressional candidates

17. Which of the following characterizes the platforms of the Democrats and Republicans?
    a. Both are essentially capitalist parties.
    b. The Republicans are capitalist, but the Democrats are not.
    c. The Republicans pledge themselves to equality, whereas the Democrats support freedom.
    d. The Republicans pledge themselves to limit all spheres of government activity, whereas the Democrats pledge themselves to increase all spheres of government activity.

18. Imagine an election in which ten legislative seats are at stake. Party A receives 60 percent of the votes cast. Party B gets 30 percent of the votes. Party C tallies 10 percent of the votes. As a result, Party A is awarded six seats; Party B, three seats; and Party C, one seat. This is an example of
    a. a proportional representation system.
    b. a majority representation system.
    c. an electoral dealignment.
    d. a first-past-the-post electoral system.

19. The most distinguishing feature of American political parties is their
    a. tight party discipline.
    b. clear ideological definition.
    c. hierarchical organization.
    d. absence of centralized power.

20. The McGovern-Fraser Commission responded to the disaffection felt by protesters during the 1968 convention by introducing
    a. procedural reforms such as affirmative action in the delegate selection process.
    b. organizational reforms enlarging the national party's role in campaign coordination.
    c. financial reforms geared toward better fund-raising and reporting.
    d. personnel reforms to allow the national organization to control the delegates' actions.

21. Compared to the United States, most democracies have all of the following *except*
    a. minor parties that regularly contest elections.
    b. minor parties that win enough votes to complicate national politics.
    c. multiparty systems.
    d. prohibitions on government funds for campaigning.

22. As far as political parties are concerned, the Constitution
    a. limits the number of major parties to two but allows an unlimited number of minor parties.
    b. limits the number of major parties to two and allows no more than ten minor parties.
    c. says nothing.
    d. provides that they be organized on the state level.

23. In 1824, Andrew Jackson received more popular and electoral votes than any other presidential candidate,
    a. but because he did not have a popular majority, the election was thrown into the House of Representatives, where he was defeated.
    b. but because he did not have an electoral majority, the election was thrown into the House of Representatives, where he was defeated.
    c. so he was declared the winner of the election.
    d. but because he did not have either a popular or an electoral majority, the election was thrown into the House of Representatives, where he won.

24. Which of these is *not* a characteristic of the responsible party model of government?
    a. Parties present clear programs to voters.
    b. Each party attempts to minimize its differences with other parties.
    c. Voters choose candidates on the basis of party.
    d. When in office, the winning party tries to carry out its program.

25. According to the text, which of the following *best* describes trends among party identifiers in America?
    a. The number of Republicans has exceeded the number of Democrats since Reagan took office in 1981.
    b. The number of Democrats has decreased, to the exclusive benefit of the Republicans.
    c. People are now more likely to call themselves independent than to identify with the two major parties.
    d. The number of Democrats has consistently exceeded the number of Republicans.

Essay Questions

1. Do you think third-party candidates play a positive role in U.S. politics rather than being a spoiler?

2. What is a "critical election"? Trace the history of the two-party system since 1860 by focusing on the three critical elections in our nation's history.

3. Is there "a dime's worth of difference" between Democrats and Republicans? Support your answer with concrete illustrations focusing on party ideologies and organization.

4. Why has the two-party system dominated American politics?

5. Discuss the functions that parties perform for the American political system.

CHAPTER 9
Nominations, Campaigns, and Elections

Learning Objectives

After reading this chapter you should be able to

- Define the key terms at the end of the chapter.
- Trace the evolution of political campaigning from being party centered to being candidate centered.
- Give a thumbnail sketch of the nominating process for Congress, state offices, and the presidency.
- Outline the changes in the presidential nominating process since 1968.
- Explain how presidential campaigns are currently financed.
- List the three basic strategies used by politic campaigns.
- Discuss the role of polling, news coverage, and political advertising in campaigns.
- Analyze the impact of split-ticket voting on American politics.
- Describe the operation of long- and short-term forces on voting choice.
- Assess whether present voting patterns are more likely to lead to pluralist or majoritarian democracy.

Nominations, Campaigns, and Elections and the Challenge of Democracy

Money is the mother's milk of politics. The difficulty for democracy occurs when economic inequality translates into political inequality. Congress began to address the problem by allowing for public financing of presidential campaigns. Candidates accept government money on the condition that they accept certain limitations as well. This practice promotes political equality. But candidates are limited in what they can spend, whereas other individuals are not. Private individuals and PACs can spend as much as they want to advertise their own views on candidates. The Supreme Court has held that limiting the expenditures of noncandidates during campaigns would be a violation of their rights to freedom of speech and expression. So the modern political campaign brings equality and freedom into conflict.

The electoral system itself has features that may make it look rather undemocratic—for example, the electoral college does make it possible for a president to be elected even though he has lost the popular vote, as in the case of George W. Bush. On the other hand, the winner-take-all system in congressional elections appears to be the essence of majoritarianism. Unlike proportional representation systems, it has the effect of leaving minorities without representation. The opening case illustrates the complexity of a U.S. presidential election, which took 36 days to count the votes in 2000 while it took just 36 hours for Canada to call a federal election, conduct the campaign, and decide the outcome.

Chapter Overview

In 1996, the Democrats and Republicans both staged carefully crafted nominating conventions that some observers thought looked more like infomercials than traditional party conventions. Meanwhile, the Reform Party experimented with a two-part nominating convention and direct balloting among party members for the presidential nomination. The contrast between these formats raises questions about the role of conventions in the nominating process in the future.

Evolution of Campaigning

Election campaigns, or organized efforts to persuade voters to choose one candidate over the others, have changed considerably over the years. In general, political parties play a much smaller role than they once did. The parties supply a label, as well as services and some funds. Candidates must campaign for their party's nomination as well as for election. Instead of relying on party organizations, however, those seeking office use the services of pollsters, political consultants, and the mass media. As a result, in the age of electronic media, campaigns have become more candidate centered than party centered.

Nominations

Unlike most other political parties in the world, American political parties usually nominate their candidates through election by party voters. For most state and local offices, candidates are chosen through primary elections of various types—*open, closed, blanket*, and *jungle*. Candidates for the presidency are chosen at national party nominating conventions. Most convention delegates are now selected in party primaries or caucuses before the convention is held. As a result, in recent years the outcome of the nominating conventions has been known long beforehand. The Iowa caucus and the New Hampshire primary have become early tests of potential candidates' appeal to party regulars and to ordinary voters. One of the characteristics of recent presidential election is the increased front-loading in the delegate selection process.

Elections

Presidents are elected indirectly, by the electoral college. Each state's number of electoral votes is equal to the size of its congressional delegation (senators plus representatives). The District of Columbia also has three votes. In most states, electoral votes are awarded on a "winner-take-all" basis. This type of election makes it possible for a candidate to win the electoral vote and the presidency while losing the popular vote. In recent years, ticket-splitting has been on the increase, and voters have tended to elect presidents from one party and members of Congress from the other party. Candidates for Congress are elected in a "first-past-the-post" system, which tends to magnify the victory margins of the winning party.

Campaigns

Candidates must pay attention to the political context of each election. It matters whether the candidate is a challenger or an incumbent. The size of the district, its voting population, and its socioeconomic makeup are also important.

Although good candidates and a strong organization are valuable resources in modern political campaigning, money is central. In recent years, Congress has moved to set strict reporting requirements for campaign contributions and created the Federal Election Commission to monitor campaign finances. Presidential nominees are eligible for public funds to support their campaigns if they agree to spend only those funds. Private individuals, political action committees, and national party committees, however, can spend unlimited amounts to promote candidates. Exploiting a loophole in the law, parties raise "soft money" to support party mailings, voter registration, and get-out-the-vote campaigns, which benefit the whole ticket and are free of the limitations on candidates. Though both parties have given lip service to the need to rewrite campaign finance laws, reform proposals such as the McCain-Feingold bill face tough going in Congress, and the cost of campaigns keeps rising.

Campaign strategies may be party centered, issue oriented, or image oriented. Candidates use a mix of polls and focus groups to design their strategies. Most campaigns emphasize using the media in two ways: through news coverage and political advertising. Each of these approaches to the media seeks the same primary goal: candidate name recognition. News coverage is often limited to brief sound bites, however. Candidates rely heavily on advertising to get before the public. Ads often contain a good deal of information, although the policy content may be deceptive or misleading. Recent elections have introduced new forms of media use. In the 2000 presidential campaign, both major party candidates appeared in the talk and entertainment shows on television targeting predominantly the female audience. The Internet allowed the candidates to communicate with activists on substantive issues, campaign appearances, requests for help, and requests for money.

Explaining Voting Choice

Voting decisions are related to both long- and short-term factors. Among long-term factors, party identification is still the most important. Candidate attributes and policy positions are both important short-term factors. Although issues still do not play the most important role in voting choices, research suggests that there is now closer alignment between voters' issue positions and their party identification. Given the importance of long-term factors in shaping voting choice, the influence of campaigns is limited. In the close election of 2000, an indefinable factor like personality worked in favor of Bush's victory.

Campaigns, Elections, and Parties

As candidates rely more on the media, American election campaigns have become highly personalized, swing states have received more attention, and party organizations have waned in importance.

Key Terms

election campaign	presidential primary	split ticket
primary election	local caucus	first-past-the-post election
closed primary	general election	open election
open primary	straight ticket	Federal Election Commission (FEC)
blanket primary		

Research and Resources

Since money is so important to political campaigning, you might want to know just where candidates get their money. One good resource is Joshua F. Goldstein's *Open Secrets: The Encyclopedia of Congressional Money & Politics* (Washington, D.C.: Congressional Quarterly Press, 1996). This work profiles members of Congress and reveals how much each received from PACs. PAC contributors are listed individually and are grouped in categories so you can find out instantly how much money a senator or representative received from business PACs, defense PACs, PACs concerned with abortion, PACs supporting Israel, and so on. The book also gives information on each Congress member's committee assignments and voting record.

For up-to-date information delivered electronically, visit the Federal Election Commission's sites at <http://www.FEC.gov/> and <http://www.tray.com/fecinfo>. These sites provide financial information about candidates, parties, and PACs. Also, try the Mojo (Mother Jones) Wire's "Coin-Operated Congress," which promises to "bring you what no print magazine can...[combining] the flexibility of the Internet with in-depth reporting to give you a unique look at what really fuels Washington"—money. The URL is <http://www.mojones.com/coinop_congress/>. The National Archives: The U.S. Electoral College and the Web site www.politics1.com provide useful background information on the electoral college.

Using Your Knowledge

1. Use on-line sources or *Open Secrets* to find out where your senators' or representatives' campaign funds came from. What proportion came from PACs? What kind of PACs provided the largest share of funds? How much money did the defeated candidate receive from PACs in the last election?

2. Visit <http://www.fec.gov/press/pacnum.jpg>. Compare the growth of corporate PACs with the growth of union PACs.

Sample Exam Questions

Multiple-Choice Questions

1. The 2000 election saw more targeting of campaign expenditures in
   a. negative ads.
   b. infomercials.
   c. swing states.
   d. large states.

2. In the contemporary American political campaign,
   a. parties play the central role.
   b. parties play a larger role than they did in the 1950s.
   c. parties provide candidates with most of their information about public opinion.
   d. candidates, rather than parties, have assumed center stage.

3. Which of the following *best* describes how U.S. candidates are usually nominated today?
   a. By party activists at conventions
   b. By party voters in primaries
   c. By all voters in primaries
   d. None of the above

4. Outside the United States, the most common means of choosing legislative candidates is
   a. by all voters in primaries.
   b. by party voters in primaries.
   c. by local party leaders, often with the approval of the national party organizations.
   d. by national party leadership.

5. Primary elections that allow voters to decide at their polling place whether to take a Republican or a Democratic ballot are called
   a. direct primaries.
   b. closed primaries.
   c. open primaries.
   d. blanket primaries.

6. Rules for selecting delegates for national party conventions
   a. are uniform throughout the nation.
   b. vary from state to state but not from party to party.
   c. vary from party to party but not from state to state.
   d. vary both from state to state and from party to party.

7. A new campaign medium making its first major appearance in the 1996 campaign was
   a. the Internet.
   b. the infomercial.
   c. the negative ad.
   d. advertising on MTV.

8. Which type of primary is *most* likely to strengthen party organization?
   a. A blanket primary
   b. An open primary
   c. A closed primary
   d. A direct primary

9. Which of these scenarios *best* characterizes the presidential nominating process today?
   a. Party dominated, many primaries, long campaigns
   b. Candidate dominated, many primaries, long campaigns
   c. Candidate dominated, few primaries, short campaigns
   d. Party dominated, few primaries, short campaigns

10. By and large, most modern candidates who win a party presidential nomination do so
    a. because their party's leaders have selected them.
    b. in spite of the preferences of most of the people who identify with their party.
    c. on their own, without help from their national party organization.
    d. because the nominating process rarely attracts more than one plausible candidate.

11. An open election means that
    a. there is no secret ballot. Votes are declared openly before an election clerk.
    b. voters decide on election day whether to take a ballot listing only Republican or only Democratic candidates.
    c. polls show a close race.
    d. there is no incumbent.

12. An argument frequently made in favor of the electoral college system is that
    a. the system it produced has been stable; alterations might result in a less stable system.
    b. it promotes majority rule.
    c. due to electoral reforms and population changes, it is no longer possible for a candidate with a minority of popular votes to win the electoral vote.
    d. does all of the above.

13. Strict campaign finance laws
    a. were passed in response to the assassination of President Garfield.
    b. were passed in response to the assassination of President Kennedy.
    c. are relatively new to American politics.
    d. have been weakened by amendments added over the years.

14. Currently, presidential election campaigns
    a. must be privately financed to hold down the federal deficit.
    b. must be entirely publicly financed under law.
    c. may receive public funds if they agree to accept and spend only those funds.
    d. must act to limit other groups wishing to promote their candidate.

15. The bill that would have banned soft money party contributions is the
    a. McCain-Feingold bill.
    b. Thompson-McCain bill.
    c. Gore-Gingrich bill.
    d. Gramm-Rudman bill.

16. Candidates for each party's nomination for president can qualify for federal funding by raising at least what amount of money?
    a. $5,000
    b. $50,000
    c. $3,000
    d. $2,000

17. An electoral strategy that stresses the candidate's experience and leadership ability would probably be considered
    a. party centered.
    b. issue oriented.
    c. image oriented.
    d. negative campaigning.

18. A party-centered strategy would be *least* appropriate in which of the following types of elections?
    a. A presidential election
    b. A senatorial election
    c. An open election
    d. A closed primary

19. Television news coverage is *least* useful in helping candidates
    a. obtain name recognition.
    b. obtain publicity while conserving campaign funds.
    c. present a detailed summary of their issue positions.
    d. publicize their current standing in the polls.

20. Public funding has all of the following effects *except*
    a. limiting campaign expenditures.
    b. equalizing the amount spent by candidates.
    c. strengthening personalized presidential campaigns.
    d. strengthening the incumbents.

21. When a voter selects candidates from different parties for different offices, the voter is said to vote a
    a. split ticket.
    b. nonpartisan ticket.
    c. party-oriented ticket.
    d. open ticket.

22. An effect of ticket-splitting has been
    a. that candidates with a minority of electoral votes may reach the White House.
    b. that candidates with a popular majority may lose their races.
    c. divided government.
    d. a move toward more closed primaries.

23. In 2000, the Supreme Court struck down California's
    a. open primary.
    b. closed primary.
    c. blanket primary.
    d. presidential primary.

24. The most important long-term force affecting U.S. elections is
    a. party identification.
    b. candidate attributes.
    c. candidate issue positions.
    d. race.

25. One can tell before the party's nominating convention who its nominee is going to be by the
    a. direct primary.
    b. front loading.
    c. campaign financing.
    d. election laws.

Essay Questions

1. Compare and contrast election systems in presidential and parliamentary form of governments. What are the advantages and disadvantages of each system?

2. How does the effort to regulate campaign finances raise the tension between freedom and equality?

3. Considering the 2000 presidential election, should the electoral college be abolished? Present the main arguments on each side of the issue.

4. The problem with Florida's voting machines raised the issue of maintaining uniformity in voting methods. What problems would be encountered in trying to obtain such uniformity?

5. Do you agree or disagree with this statement: "Presidential elections are no longer contests between candidates; they are battles among media teams"? Explain the reasons for your position.

CHAPTER 10
Interest Groups

Learning Objectives

After reading this chapter you should be able to

- Define the key terms at the end of the chapter.
- Outline the positive and negative roles played by interest groups in American politics.
- Explain how interest groups form.
- Create a profile of the kind of person most likely to be represented by an interest group.
- Describe the major resources that interest groups use to influence policy.
- List the tactics used by interest groups to win the support of policymakers.
- Account for the recent increase in the number of interest groups.
- Discuss the impact of high-tech lobbying by interest groups.

Interest Groups and the Challenge of Democracy

The failure of the WTO meeting in Seattle represents a triumph of the forces of pluralism over the forces of majoritarianism demanding more efficiency and free trade. The case reflects the efforts of the pluralist forces to combat globalism.

The founders anticipated that factions or interest groups would play an important part in politics. James Madison's writings show that they believed factions would thrive in an atmosphere of freedom: "Liberty is to faction what air is to fire." The only way to eliminate factions or interest-group politics was to curtail freedom. The founders were certainly not prepared to abandon the very value for which they had fought the Revolutionary War. So they proposed using factions to combat factions, with the government serving as the mediator.

More recently, pluralist political scientists have resurrected these Madisonian hopes. They have made it clear that American politics is not majoritarian but has interest groups at its center. They also expect interests to counterbalance one another and for the system to provide open access. However, as this chapter indicates, some interests, notably those of business, are much better represented than others. Opportunities for access may often depend on money. The fact that there are no "poor PACs" and no "food stamp PACs" suggests that the interests of the poor may not be adequately represented. Insofar as political equality means "one person, one vote," Americans are pretty much equal; but if political equality means more than that, then it follows that where contemporary interest group politics are concerned, social inequality leads to political inequality.

So why not limit the activities of interest groups to promote open access and make pluralism function as Madison expected it would? The answer is that limiting interest groups also means limiting the right of the people to petition their government—a fundamental freedom guaranteed under the Constitution.

Chapter Overview

Interest Groups and the American Political Tradition

Interest groups, or lobbies—organized bodies of individuals who share some political goals and try to influence policy decisions—have always been a part of American politics. The Constitution itself was designed to preserve freedom by relying on what we now call pluralist politics, or, in Madisonian terms, the use of factions to counteract other factions. But giving people freedom to organize does not necessarily promote political equality. Thus, the value people place on equality may determine whether they believe that interest groups are bad or good.

Interest groups perform a variety of important functions in the American system: they represent their members to the government; they provide channels for citizen participation; they educate their members, government officials, and the public at large; they build the public agenda by putting issues before the government; and they monitor programs important to their members.

How Interest Groups Form

Modern pluralists believe that interest groups further democracy. They believe interest groups form naturally by a process similar to the "invisible hand" in economics. When unorganized people are adversely affected by change, they organize themselves into groups to protect their interests. Yet empirical evidence suggests that this doesn't always happen—more than a simple disturbance is required. Strong leadership—provided by interest-group entrepreneurs—may be critically important; in addition, social class is also a factor in interest-group formation. Although the poor and less educated do form groups to advance their interests, middle- and upper-class individuals are much more likely to see the value of interest groups and to organize.

Interest Group Resources

An interest group's strength and effectiveness usually depends on its resources. These resources include members, lobbyists, and money. Interest groups work hard to build their memberships and to combat the "free rider" problem. They also keep their members well informed of group activities. Lobbyists, preferably Washington insiders with previous government experience, present the group's views to legislators and officials of the executive branch. Currently, an important resource used by interest groups is the political action committee (PAC). This type of organization enables a group to more easily make political campaign contributions in the hope of obtaining better access to officials. PACs may make influence a function of money (thereby reducing political equality), but limiting PACs would amount to a restriction on freedom of expression. Furthermore, PACs also allow small givers to pool their resources to obtain more clout.

Lobbying Tactics

Interest groups may seek help from the legislature, the courts, or the administration. Lobbyists carry out their task in several ways. They may use direct lobbying aimed at policymakers themselves—through legal advocacy, personal presentations, or committee testimony. Alternatively, they may rely on grassroots lobbying by enlisting group members to pressure elected officials through letters or political protests. Lobbyists may also use information campaigns, bringing their views to the attention of the general public through public relations methods. These campaigns may involve publicizing the voting records of legislators or sponsoring research. Lobbyists may also use e-mail, fax machines, and the Internet as high-tech tools of the trade. Finally, lobbyists may lobby for each other through coalition building.

Is the System Biased?

Are the decisions made in a pluralist system fair? Perhaps, if all significant interests are represented by lobbying groups and the government listens to the views of all major interests as it makes policy. Yet research shows that interest groups have a membership bias—some parts of society are better organized than others. But, in addition to groups motivated by the self-interest of their members, there are also citizen groups or public interest groups motivated for reasons other than economic self-interest; these groups seek to achieve a common good that benefits all citizens. Initially, most of these groups were liberal. Recently, there has been a growth of citizen groups, who are organized on policy concerns unrelated to members' vocational interests. Organizations pursuing environmental protection, consumer protection, good government, family values, and equality for various groups have grown in number. These groups receive a significant coverage in the national press on their issues.

Although the First Amendment guarantees the right to organize as a central part of American politics, interest groups may confer unacceptable advantages on some segments of the community. Thus, some efforts have been made to limit their impact, through federal regulation of lobbying, disclosure laws, gift bans, and public financing of presidential campaigns.

Key Terms

interest group	entrepreneur	grassroots lobbying
lobby	free rider problem	information campaign
lobbyist	trade association	coalition building
agenda building	political action committee (PAC)	membership bias
program monitoring	direct lobbying	citizen groups

Research and Resources

One of the most significant recent developments in American politics has been the proliferation of PACs. There are a number of useful reference works on PACs. The following two publications are particularly valuable.

Congressional Quarterly. *CQ's Federal PAC Directory. 1998-99*. Washington, D.C.: Congressional Quarterly Press, 1998.

Zuckerman, Ed, ed. *The Almanac of Federal PACs: 1998-99*. Washington, D.C.: Amward, 1998. Provides up-to-date descriptions of the interests and orientations of individual PACs, along with a record of their recent giving activities.

Check Yahoo for an extensive index of interest groups arranged by subject at <http://www.yahoo.com/Business_and_Economy/Organizations/Public_Interest_Groups>. Some lobbying firms describe the services they offer. For a list, try <http://www.yahoo.com/Business_and_Economy/Companies/Government/Lobbying/>. Here are Web sites for a few well-known interest groups: the American Medical Association at <http://www.ama-assn.org/>, the National Organization for Women at <http://www.now.org>, the National Rifle Association at <http://www.nra.org>, the Children's Defense Fund at <tmn.com/cdf/index.html>, and the Christian Coalition at <http://www.cc.org>.

Using Your Knowledge

1. Visit the Web sites of two or three interest groups. What types of information do they offer? What online strategies do they use to mobilize members?

2. Visit the sites of some of the lobbying firms listed on Yahoo. What types of services do they offer to their clients?

Getting Involved

There are plenty of opportunities to learn more about the Washington community and the think tanks and lobbyists that play such an important role in policymaking. The list provided here will give you some idea of the range of possibilities available.

Internships at Think Tanks

The American Enterprise Institute (AEI) assigns interns to work for resident scholars specializing in economic policy, foreign and defense policy, or social and political policy. Internships are available in the fall, spring, or summer and run twelve weeks. They are unpaid. Deadlines are September 1 for fall, December 1 for spring, and April 1 for summer. For further information, contact the American Enterprise Institute, Intern Coordinator, 1150 Seventeenth St., NW, Washington, D.C. 20036. Telephone: (202) 862-5800.

The Brookings Institution assigns its unpaid interns to work on research involving political institutions, processes, and policies. Internships run twelve weeks and are available in the fall, spring, and summer. Deadlines are August 1 for fall, December 1 for spring, and April 1 for summer. Write to the Brookings Institution, Internship Coordinator, 1775 Massachusetts Ave., NW, Washington, D.C. 20036. Find Brookings on-line at <http://www.brook.edu/>.

Common Cause uses interns to work for grassroots lobbying efforts in the states as well as to monitor congressional meetings and do other research. Write to the Common Cause, Volunteer Office, 2030 M Street, NW, Washington, D.C. 20036. Telephone: (202) 833-1200. You can even apply on-line at <http://www.commoncause.org/about/intern_intro.htm>.

Internships with Interest Groups

The Feminist Majority Foundation offers women and men the chance to lobby for women's issues, including reproductive rights, sexual harassment, and women's rights. Student interns may work in the Washington, D.C. or Los Angeles offices. For details, contact the Fund for Feminist Majority, 8105 West Third St., Suite 1, Los Angeles, CA 90048, dgarcia@aol.com or 1600 Wilson Boulevard, Suite 801, Arlington, VA 22209, <intern@feminist.org>. Telephone: (703) 522-2214.

Americans for Democratic Action, long the nation's best-known liberal organization, offers full- and part-time internships during the school year; there is no pay, but hours are flexible, and arrangements may be made with home institutions for coordinating course credit. Contact Americans for Democratic Action, 1625 K Street, Suite 210, Washington, D.C. 20005. Telephone: (202) 785-5980. The ADA Web site is <http://www.adaction.org>.

The Union of Concerned Scientists involves students in research and lobbying on issues related to arms control and the impact of technology. The internships are paid, and thirty to forty hours of work per week is the normal expectation. For further information, contact the Union of Concerned Scientists, 1616 P Street, NW, Suite 310, Washington, D.C. 20036. Telephone: (202) 332-0900. See their Web site at <http://www.ucsusa.org/join/internship.html>.

The National Taxpayers Union works for lower taxes and reduced government spending. It offers paid internships to students interested in working on researching taxpayer issues, preparing a congressional spending analysis, and lobbying at the grassroots, national, and state levels. Students should apply six weeks ahead of the desired starting date and by April 1 for summer internships. For further information, contact the Internship Program, National Taxpayers Union, 325 Pennsylvania Avenue, SE, Washington, D.C. 20002. Telephone: (703) 683-5700. Find out more on-line at <http://www.ntu.org/> or e-mail <dircksen@ntu.org>.

Sample Exam Questions

Multiple-Choice Questions

1. According to Tocqueville,
   a. lobbies are undemocratic.
   b. Americans had difficulty organizing themselves.
   c. Americans' tendency to join associations reflected a strong democratic culture.
   d. "liberty is to faction what air is to fire."

2. Few interest groups rely on paid TV advertising as their primary weapon in advocacy campaigns, because
   a. FCC regulations mandate equal time for all viewpoints.
   b. ads are expensive and their impact is limited.
   c. commissioned research is more persuasive.
   d. of all of the above.

3. The idea that interest groups originate when unorganized people are adversely affected by change
   a. is called the disturbance theory.
   b. was proven by the experience of people living in the West End of Boston.
   c. is a rejection of pluralist theory.
   d. is a realist view of interest-group formation.

4. The development of the United Farm Workers Union is a good example of
   a. the invisible-hand theory of interest-group formation.
   b. the importance of interest-group leadership.
   c. the relationship of social class to interest-group formation.
   d. all of the above.

5. Which of the following is an example of a public interest group?
   a. The Business Roundtable
   b. The National Rifle Association
   c. The AFL-CIO
   d. The Children's Defense Fund

6. Interest groups in political systems with low scores run the risk of being co-opted by policymakers because of their
   a. partnership with the government.
   b. opposition to the government.
   c. negligible size.
   d. positive attitude.

7. Political action committees
   a. have no limits on the money they may contribute to candidates.
   b. rarely reflect the interests of ideological groups.
   c. are a method of using money to gain access to public officials.
   d. promote political equality.

8. Most PAC contributions come from
   a. business groups and trade associations.
   b. citizens' groups.
   c. women's groups.
   d. unions.

9. The *most* commonly used direct lobbying tactic is
   a. the personal presentation of a group's position.
   b. the letter-writing campaign.
   c. testifying at committee hearings.
   d. legal advocacy.

10. The *most* commonly used tactic of grassroots lobbying is
    a. letter writing.
    b. legal advocacy.
    c. political protest.
    d. newspaper advertising.

11. Who would most likely belong to a group working to advance their interests?
     a. People receiving veterans' benefits
     b. AFDC recipients
     c. Food stamp recipients
     d. People receiving Medicaid

12. Coalitions formed for lobbying purposes
     a. tend to be informal, ad hoc arrangements.
     b. usually waste resources.
     c. are prohibited under federal law.
     d. generally center around long-term goals and broad issue areas.

13. A major difference between public interest groups and other lobbies is that public interest groups
     a. do not generally pursue the economic self-interests of their members.
     b. are always poorly funded.
     c. do not support conservative causes.
     d. still rely primarily on grassroots tactics.

14. The Web is instrumental in building
     a. government support.
     b. new advocacy organizations.
     c. opposition to the government.
     d. new political systems.

15. All of the following contributed to the increase of business lobbies in Washington *except*
     a. the expanded scope of federal government activity.
     b. the competitive nature of business lobbying.
     c. the success of interest groups on the religious right.
     d. the success of liberal public interest groups.

16. As the American system becomes increasingly centered around interest-group advocacy,
     a. majoritarian democracy is enhanced.
     b. political parties are strengthened.
     c. business has an advantage.
     d. interest groups take on all the functions formerly associated with political parties.

17. Which of these is *not* a tactic commonly used in direct lobbying?
     a. Meeting with members of Congress
     b. Meeting with congressional staff
     c. Testifying at congressional hearings
     d. Direct mail campaigns

18. Which of these applies to former legislators and their staffers?
     a. They may begin direct lobbying of former colleagues immediately.
     b. They may begin direct lobbying of former colleagues after a six-month "cooling-off period."
     c. They may begin direct lobbying of former colleagues after a one-year "cooling-off period."
     d. They are strictly prohibited from lobbying.

19. According to James Madison, interest groups were
     a. natural, but their effects could be controlled.
     b. unnatural and could be eliminated.
     c. natural but could be eliminated by establishing democratic institutions.
     d. unnatural and would never form in America.

20. According to the text, lobbyists
    a. are poorly paid.
    b. have often had previous government service.
    c. must be lawyers.
    d. rely mainly on arm-twisting and back-slapping to get their way.

21. The reason Christian lobbies have fared so poorly is that they are built
    a. almost entirely on direct mail.
    b. to press for conservative causes.
    c. on electronic technology.
    d. around the 1980s.

22. Citizen groups have good credibility because they are
    a. well organized.
    b. not motivated by financial gain.
    c. large organizations.
    d. well financed.

23. A PAC that has no parent lobbying organization and is used to channel campaign funds is
    a. illegal.
    b. a nonconnected PAC.
    c. a free rider.
    d. an arm twister.

24. Which of the following variables is frequently used to explain interest-group formation?
    a. Change in the environment
    b. Leadership
    c. Class
    d. All of the above

25. Today, the most heavily unionized sector of the U.S. economy is the
    a. industrial sector.
    b. service sector.
    c. computer industry.
    d. government sector.

Essay Questions

1. Explain the conflicts between the forces of pluralism and majoritarianism on the issue of the WTO.

2. What benefits do interest groups provide to the American political system?

3. Describe the key variables that explain interest-group success. Give examples to justify your choices.

4. How has the growth of interest-group activity in Washington affected the tension between pluralism and majoritarianism?

5. "On the whole, PACs are detrimental to democracy." Explain why you agree or disagree with this statement.

CHAPTER 11
Congress

Learning Objectives

After reading this chapter you should be able to

- Define the key terms at the end of the chapter.
- Outline the constitutional duties of the House and Senate.
- Account for the factors in congressional election.
- Describe the characteristics of a typical member of Congress.
- Sketch the processes by which a bill becomes a law and an issue is placed on the congressional agenda.
- Explain the importance of the committee system in the legislative process.
- Distinguish between congressional rules of procedure and norms of behavior.
- List several important sources of legislative voting cues.
- Explain the dilemma that representatives face in choosing between trustee and delegate roles.
- Evaluate the extent to which the structure of Congress promotes pluralist or majoritarian politics.

Congress and the Challenge of Democracy

The structure of Congress, both as it was designed by the founders and as it has evolved over the past two centuries, heightens the tension between pluralism and majoritarianism in American politics. Under the Constitution, the system of checks and balances divides complete lawmaking power between Congress and the president. In addition, members of Congress are elected from particular states or congressional districts and ultimately depend upon their constituents to re-elect them. Two facts suggest majoritarian influence on Congress. First, to become law, legislation must be passed by a majority vote in each house. Second, in recent years at least, the party system, which may act as a majoritarian influence on politics, has had a greater impact on the way members actually vote. Considering the thin Republican majority in the House and the evenly split Senate resulting from the election of 2000, Congress will likely be more pluralistic in order to pass legislation on key issues faced by the nation.

Much about the structure of Congress reinforces pluralism. The committee structure encourages members of Congress to gain expertise in narrow policy areas. The experience members gain in these areas often leads them to look after particular constituencies or special interests. Furthermore, since the outcome of the legislative process is usually the result of vote trading, logrolling, bargaining, and coalition building, any final product is likely to represent all sorts of concessions to various interests.

Chapter Overview

The Origin and Powers of Congress

The U.S. Congress is a bicameral (two-house) legislature. Its basic structure grew out of the Great Compromise at the Constitutional Convention. As a result of that compromise, each state is represented in the upper house (or Senate) by two senators, who serve staggered six-year terms; in the lower house (the House of Representatives), states are represented according to their population. Members of the lower house serve two-year terms. In 1929, the total number of representatives was fixed at 435. Whenever the population shifts (as demonstrated by a decennial census), the country's 435 single-member legislative districts must be reapportioned to reflect the changes and provide equal representation.

Duties of the House and Senate

The Constitution gives the House and Senate shared powers, including the power to declare war, raise an army and navy, borrow and coin money, regulate interstate commerce, create federal courts, establish rules for the naturalization of immigrants, and "make all laws which shall be necessary and proper for carrying into Execution the foregoing Powers."

However, there are some differences between the House and Senate in their constitutional responsibilities. All revenue bills must originate in the House. The House has the power of impeachment and the power formally to charge the president, vice president, and other "civil Officers" of the national government with serious crimes. The Senate is empowered to act as a court to try impeachment, with the chief justice of the Supreme Court presiding. The Constitution gives the Senate some additional powers, such as approving presidential nominations including all federal judges, ambassadors, and cabinet members. The Constitution gives the president the power to negotiate treaties with foreign countries. The Senate must approve any treaty with a two-thirds majority.

Electing the Congress

Although elections offer voters the opportunity to express their approval or disapproval of congressional performance, voters rarely reject House incumbents. Polls show that the public lacks confidence in Congress as a whole and supports term limits; but on the other hand, most people are satisfied with their own particular legislator. Incumbents have enormous advantages that help them keep their seats. For example, incumbents are generally much more attractive to PACs and find it easier to obtain funds for re-election campaigns. Incumbents usually have greater name recognition; they acquire this name recognition by using their franking privileges and building a reputation for handling casework. Gerrymandering during redistricting may also work to the benefit of an incumbent. Senate races tend to be more competitive than House races; incumbency is less of an advantage in the Senate, partly because of the greater visibility of challengers in Senate races. When challengers do defeat incumbents, it is often the case that the previous election was close or the ideology and party identification of the state's voters favor the challenger.

Members of Congress tend to be white, male professionals with college or graduate degrees. There are relatively few women and minority-group members in Congress. To remedy this situation, some people favor descriptive representation; others argue that devices such as racial gerrymandering discriminate unjustly against white candidates. Recent court decisions have dealt setbacks to racial gerrymandering.

How Issues Get on the Congressional Agenda

Although many issues on the congressional agenda seem to be perennial, new issues do emerge. Sometimes a crisis or visible event prompts Congress to act; at other times, congressional champions of particular proposals are able to win powerful supporters for their ideas. Congressional leaders and committee chairpersons also have the power to place items on the congressional agenda, and they often do so in response to interest groups.

The Dance of Legislation

Bills become laws by a process that is simple in its outline. A bill may be introduced in either house. It is then assigned to a specialized committee, which may refer it to a subcommittee for closer study and modification. When the subcommittee has completed its work, it may send the proposal back to the full committee, which may then approve it and report it out to the chamber for debate, amendment, or a vote on passage.

Actual floor procedures in the two houses differ substantially. In the House, the Rules Committee specifies the form of debate. In contrast, the Senate works within a tradition of unlimited debate and unanimous consent petitions. If a bill passes the two houses in different versions, the differences must be reconciled in a conference committee, and the bill must then be passed in its new form by each house. Once the bill has passed Congress, it is sent to the president for his signature, veto, or pocket veto. The pocket veto can be used only when Congress adjourns. Congress approved a line-item veto that allowed the president to invalidate particular sections of bills, but the Supreme Court declared it unconstitutional.

Committees: The Workhorses of Congress

The real work of lawmaking happens in the legislative committees. One of the reasons for the committee system is division of labor. The American system of specialized standing committees allows members of Congress to build up expertise in issue areas as they build up seniority in Congress. Standing committees are broken down into subcommittees that allow members to acquire even more specialized expertise. Subcommittee members are often the dominant forces shaping legislation. In addition to their work on standing committees, members of Congress serve on joint committees made up of legislators from both houses; select committees established to deal with special issues; and conference committees, which work out differences between versions of legislation passed by the two houses. Leadership on committees is linked to seniority (although members have the option of secret ballot).

Committee hearings represent an important stage in drafting legislation and are often used by legislators as ways of gaining publicity on an issue. Committees themselves differ in terms of style. Some work by consensus; others are more conflictive.

Oversight: Following Through on Legislation

In addition to its responsibility for passing new laws, Congress must also keep watch over the administration of existing laws. Through this oversight function, Congress is able to monitor existing policies and programs to see if agencies are carrying them out as Congress intended. Oversight occurs in a variety of ways, including hearings, formal reports, and informal contacts between congressional and agency personnel. Since the 1970s, Congress has increased its oversight over the executive branch. Generally, it has done so in an effort to find ways to make programs run better; sometimes it tends to become involved in petty details, making itself vulnerable to the charge of micromanagement.

Reliance on a committee system decentralizes power and makes American democracy more pluralistic; yet there is a majoritarian aspect as well, since most committees approximate the general profile of the parties' congressional membership, and legislation must still receive a majority vote in each house before becoming law.

Leaders and Followers in Congress

Each house has leaders who work to maximize their party's influence and keep their chamber functioning smoothly and efficiently. Party leadership in the House is exercised by the speaker of the House and the minority leader. In the Senate, power is vested in the majority and minority leaders. These four leaders are selected by vote of their own party members in the chamber. Much of their work consists of persuasion and coalition building.

Rules and Norms of Behavior

An important difference between the two chambers is in the House's use of its Rules Committee, which serves as the "traffic cop" governing the floor debate. Lacking a similar committee, the Senate relies on unanimous consent agreement to govern the rules of debate. Moreover, unlike the House, the Senate has the power to call for a filibuster to prolong the debate on an issue.

Each house has its own formal rules of procedure specifying how debates are conducted in that chamber. In addition, each house also has unwritten, informal norms of behavior that help reduce conflict among people who often hold strongly opposing points of view but who must work together. Some norms, such as the apprenticeship norm, have been weakened; but, over time, successful members of Congress still learn to compromise to build support for measures that interest them.

The Legislative Environment

Legislators look to four sources for their cues on how to vote on issues. First, rank-and-file party members usually try to support their party when they can, and partisanship has increased in recent years as each of the major parties has become more homogeneous. Second, the president is often actively engaged in trying to persuade legislators to vote his way. The views of the constituents back home are a third factor in how legislators vote. Finally, interest groups provide legislators with information on issues and their impact on the home district. These four influences push Congress in both the majoritarian and the pluralist direction.

The Dilemma of Representation

Every member of Congress lives in two worlds: the world of presidents and the world of personalized shopping bags. Each member of Congress has to deal with the demands of Washington politics and the politics of his/her home district or state. A central question for representative government is whether representatives should act as trustees who vote according to their consciences or as delegates who vote as their constituents wish them to vote. In the U.S. Congress, members feel a responsibility to both roles. A need to consider the larger national interest pushes them to act as trustees, while the need to face their constituents at the next election leads them to act more like delegates. By and large, members of Congress do not consistently adopt one role or the other.

Pluralism, Majoritarianism, and Democracy

The American Congress contrasts sharply with the legislatures in parliamentary democracies. Strong party systems and a lack of checks and balances to block government action make parliamentary democracies more majoritarian. Congress's decentralization, plus the lack of a strong party system, make Congress an institution better suited to pluralist democracy. Moreover, the United States with an increasing diversity of economic, social, religious, and racial groups will influence Congress to be more pluralistic.

Key Terms

reapportionment	pocket veto	speaker of the House
impeachment	line-item veto	majority leader
incumbent	standing committee	filibuster
gerrymandering	joint committee	cloture
casework	select committee	constituents
descriptive representation	conference committee	trustee
racial gerrymandering	seniority	delegate
veto	oversight	parliamentary system
pluralism		

Research and Resources

For research on Congress, a useful starting point is *Congressional Quarterly's Guide to Congress*, 4th ed. (Washington, D.C.: Congressional Quarterly Press, 1991). This work includes information on the origins and development of Congress, its powers and procedures, and the qualifications and conduct of its members. In addition, there are sections on Congress, the electorate, and on pressures on Congress within our system. Finally, the volume contains a biographical index of every member of Congress from 1789 on.

Two other *Congressional Quarterly* publications, *Congress and the Nation* (mentioned in the Preface) and *Politics in America*, are also helpful to those studying Congress. Editions of the latter work are published biennially and provide state-by-state summaries of current political issues as well as biographies of all current members of Congress, their interest group ratings, PAC support, committee memberships, and votes on key issues. The interest group ratings of members of Congress may also be found on-line using "Voter Information Services" at <http://world.std.com/~voteinfo/>.

Congressional Quarterly also provides up-to-the-minute information through its Web sites. You can keep track of the recent activities of individual members of Congress at "CQ's On the Job," <http://voter96. cqalert.com/cq_job.htm>. You can track voting outcomes on specific bills at *Congressional Quarterly's* VoteWatch, <http://pathfinder.com/CQ/>. Another useful source on Congress can be found at <http:// congress.org/main.html>. This site is sponsored by Issue Dynamics and Capital Advantage, two Washington firms that claim "expertise in communicating with Congress." A third useful site is sponsored by *Rollcall*, the newspaper of Capitol Hill, and bills itself as "the premiere Web site for news and information about Congress." You will find it at <http://www.rollcall1.com/>.

What if these sources do not provide enough information for your purposes? Suppose you need to find the actual text of a Senate floor debate or a House committee hearing? You'll want to turn to government documents. Floor debates are covered in the *Congressional Record*, published daily while Congress is in session and available on-line. To access it, try "Thomas," the congressional Web site maintained by the Library of Congress at <http://thomas.loc.gov/>. The University of California's GPOGate allows you to search a variety of types of government documents on-line, including the daily *Congressional Record* from 1994 on. Instructions for searching the *Congressional Record* may be found at <http://www.gpo.ucop.edu/ hints/cong_record.html>. Another useful source is http:www.congress.gov.

One other important resource for research on Congress is the *Congressional Quarterly Almanac*.

Using Your Knowledge

1. Using *Congressional Quarterly's Weekly Reports* or the Internet resources suggested above, trace the legislation history of a bill passed by Congress in the last two years. When was the bill introduced? What were its major provisions? What committees examined it? Were there any major changes made by committees? What were they? Were there major amendments voted on during the floor debate?

2. Now, for a more extensive version of the above project, look up the House and Senate committee hearings on the bill. Who testified on behalf of the legislation? Who opposed it? What were the major arguments advanced by proponents and their opposition? Next, find the floor debates on the bill in the *Congressional Record*. Who supported the bill? Who opposed it? Why?

3. How does your representative fare in the ratings by Americans for Democratic Action? The Christian Coalition? The American Conservative Union? The AFL-CIO? How does your representative stand on the Contract with America? Use the Web sites suggested above to find the answers to these questions.

4. Watch a House debate and a Senate debate on C-SPAN. What differences do you notice between the two? Next, watch a committee hearing. Describe the differences between committee hearings and floor debates.

Getting Involved

If you would like to have a chance to learn more about the life of a representative or senator, you might begin by contacting your own congressional representatives. They may welcome part-time volunteer help in their offices in the home district, or they may have internships available in their Washington offices. The Internet puts tremendous resources for finding congressional internships at your fingertips; just visit <http:/www.senate.gov>, and perform a search using the term "internships" and you'll find a wealth of information at your disposal.

Roll Call, the weekly "local" newspaper covering Congress that circulates on Capitol Hill, offers internships. These internships are unpaid and last at least three months. For further information, contact *Roll Call*, 201 Massachusetts Ave., NE, Washington, D.C. 20002. Find them on-line at <http://www.rollcall.com>.

Sample Exam Questions

Multiple-Choice Questions

1. While drafting the Constitution in 1787, the fiercest struggle for power centered on
   a. representation in the legislature.
   b. election of the president.
   c. federal or unitary structure.
   d. the power of the Senate.

2. Incumbents are generally more likely than their challengers to have all of the following advantages *except*
   a. greater name recognition.
   b. White House support.
   c. greater attractiveness to campaign contributors.
   d. a staff doing casework for constituents.

3. Elected officials are drawn disproportionately from the ranks of
   a. college-educated white males.
   b. professional women.
   c. Hispanics.
   d. blue-collar white males.

4. When a president vetoes a bill,
   a. it cannot be reconsidered in that session of Congress.
   b. it becomes law if it can be repassed by at least three-fourths of the membership of each house.
   c. it becomes law if it can be repassed by at least two-thirds of those voting in each house.
   d. it becomes law if it can be repassed by a simple majority in each house.

5. Traditionally, the Senate allows unlimited debate on measures before it votes, but there is a procedure for ending debate. That procedure is called a
   a. cloture vote.
   b. germaneness rule.
   c. unanimous consent agreement.
   d. filibuster.

6. The legislative agenda is shaped by
   a. the president.
   b. party leaders and committee chairs.
   c. new issues and events.
   d. all of the above.

7. A permanent committee specializing in a particular area of legislative policy is called a
   a. standing committee.
   b. steering committee.
   c. select committee.
   d. conference committee.

8. Both the House and the Senate share many important powers *except* the power to
   a. declare war.
   b. raise an army.
   c. regulate interstate commerce.
   d. ratify treaties.

9. Which of the following is *true* about partisanship in Congress?
   a. Partisanship is always more pronounced in the House than in the Senate.
   b. Partisanship was greater in the mid-1990s than in the late 1960s.
   c. The most recent figures show greater partisanship in the House than in the Senate.
   d. As the importance of party identification has declined in the electorate, so has partisanship in Congress.

10. On congressional committees, the chair is usually occupied by
    a. the senior minority member.
    b. the senior majority member.
    c. a member selected by all committee members in an open, democratic process.
    d. a member from the most populous state.

11. The Supreme Court forced a redrawing of racially gerrymandered districts. In the 1996 election, the result was that
    a. racial polarization led to the defeat of minority members.
    b. racial polarization led to the victory of minority members.
    c. advantages of incumbency outweighed race and minority candidates were re-elected.
    d. most minority candidates refused to seek re-election.

12. Which of the following features of the committee system tend to make it more of a pluralist than a majoritarian device?
    a. Decentralization
    b. Specialization
    c. Congressional attention to the interests of the district
    d. All of the above

13. In the Senate, the greatest power resides in the office of
    a. majority leader.
    b. minority leader.
    c. vice president.
    d. president pro tempore.

14. To convict a president of impeachment, what portion of the Senate's vote is necessary?
    a. A simple majority
    b. A two-thirds majority
    c. A three-fourths majority
    d. None of the above

15. The reasons Senate challengers have a higher success rate than House challengers include all of the following *except*
    a. they are higher quality candidates.
    b. they are often governors or members of the House.
    c. they can attract significant campaign funds.
    d. they are supported by the party's national committee.

16. Redrawing the boundaries of an electoral district in an irregular shape to favor a particular party or candidate is called
    a. logrolling.
    b. gerrymandering.
    c. pairing.
    d. filibustering.

17. When a member of Congress decides to follow his conscience and votes for legislation limiting the availability of abortion under Medicaid, which of the following *best* accounts for his choice?
    a. The theory of majoritarianism
    b. The idea of descriptive representation
    c. The view of representatives as delegates
    d. The view of representatives as trustees

18. Members of Congress take voting cues from which of the following?
    a. Interest groups
    b. Political parties
    c. Constituents
    d. All of the above

19. The common name for the process of reviewing agency operations to determine whether an agency is carrying out policies as Congress intended is called
    a. oversight.
    b. legislative review.
    c. judicial review.
    d. germaneness.

20. Under a parliamentary system,
    a. divided government is common.
    b. the chief executive is directly elected by the people.
    c. the leader of the majority party usually heads the government.
    d. legislators are chosen through proportional representation.

21. The number of representatives to which states are entitled in the House of Representatives
    a. was fixed permanently when each state joined the Union.
    b. changes to reflect voter turnout in each election.
    c. is revised every five years based on the quinquennial census.
    d. is revised every ten years based on the decennial census.

22. Which of the following actions is *not* specifically authorized in the Constitution?
    a. The president uses the line-item veto to reject part of a bill.
    b. The president signs a bill into law.
    c. The president vetoes a bill.
    d. The president "pocket vetoes" a bill by failing to sign it at the end of a legislative session.

23. Impeachment is a power
    a. to charge an official with treason, bribery, or other high crimes or misdemeanors.
    b. to try an official charged with treason, bribery, or other high crimes or misdemeanors.
    c. to remove from office an official convicted of treason, bribery, or other high crimes or misdemeanors.
    d. that has not been used in this century.

24. Which committee settles the differences between the House and the Senate?
    a. Conference Committee
    b. Standing Committee
    c. Subcommittee
    d. Select Committee

25. Rules are decided in the Senate by
    a. the Rules Committee
    b. the majority leader
    c. the vice president
    d. a unanimous consent agreement.

Essay Questions

1. What advantages does incumbency give a member of the House of Representatives? Is incumbency as great an advantage to senators? Why or why not?

2. Some people have argued that to be truly representative, a legislature should mirror the characteristics of the people he or she is supposed to represent. Is the American Congress representative in this sense? Give specific examples concerning the extent to which Congress mirrors the general population with respect to race, gender, education, and occupational status.

3. Does the congressional committee system, as it now operates, better fit the pluralist or majoritarian model of democracy?

4. What major influences help legislators decide how to vote on particular issues?

5. Distinguish between the trustee and delegate roles of representatives. Which role, if either, tends to be more characteristic of American legislators?

6. How does a bill become law?

7. How does the European Parliament work?

CHAPTER 12
The Presidency

Learning Objectives

After reading this chapter you should be able to

- Define the key terms at the end of the chapter.
- List the powers and duties of the president, as set forth in the Constitution.
- Describe other sources that presidents have used to expand the authority of the office.
- Explain why presidential popularity usually declines while a president is in office.
- Outline the process by which presidents are elected.
- Explain why modern presidents are more likely to rely on the White House staff than on the cabinet for advice on policymaking.
- Explain what is meant by referring to the president as "chief lobbyist."
- Point out the assets and liabilities a president brings with him as he tries to translate his political vision into public policy.
- Describe the special skills presidents need for crisis management.
- Discuss the role of presidential character in evaluating presidential candidates.

The Presidency and the Challenge of Democracy

The opening case illustrates the difficulty President Bush faces in building a majority to pass his legislative policy preferences. Realizing his unusual victory and almost evenly divided Congress, he emphasizes uniting the Democrats and the Republicans.

The president and vice president are the only nationally elected political officials in the United States. As a result, there is strong moral pressure on the president to be "the president of all the people." The president is potentially the focal point of majoritarian politics in the American system. He is in a unique position to see that the national interest is not always the sum of all our single or special interests. Following opinion polls may make him aware of the need to appeal to the majority. Yet, the realities of American presidential politics are more pluralistic than majoritarian. Although classical majoritarian theory might put a premium on being responsible to "the people," the reality of presidential politics is that people to whom presidents respond are organized in groups.

Chapter Overview

The task of designing the office of chief executive presented the founders with a dilemma. They had just rebelled against a king and were naturally reluctant to concentrate too much power in the hands of one individual. Yet, their experience under the Articles of Confederation convinced them that strong national leadership was needed. So they established the office of president—a position filled by one person chosen independently of Congress by indirect election through the electoral college. To limit presidential power, they relied on two things: the mechanism of checks and balances and their expectation that the anticipated first incumbent, George Washington, would set good precedents.

The Constitutional Basis of Presidential Power

According to the Constitution, the president is the administrative head of the nation and the commander-in-chief of the armed forces. He has the power to convene Congress and to grant pardons. Subject to various congressional limitations, he may veto legislation passed by Congress; appoint ambassadors, judges, cabinet members, and other key officials; and make treaties.

The Expansion of Presidential Power

The list of the president's constitutional powers does not tell the whole story, however. Presidential power has increased tremendously since the Constitution was adopted. The expansion of presidential power resulted from claims that the president has certain inherent powers implied by the Constitution, such as the power to remove cabinet officers. In addition, Congress has also delegated power to the executive branch, allowing the president more freedom to implement policies.

Yet, the president's ability to persuade is one of the most important factors determining how much power he has. His persuasiveness is often related to his personality but may also result from his reputation and prestige. These attributes, in turn, spring from such things as past successes (at the polls or with Congress) and presidential popularity. Presidential popularity may be affected by many factors, including economic conditions, wars, and unanticipated events. Presidents usually are at the peak of their popularity during the "honeymoon period" of their first year in office, and they monitor their popularity closely as a kind of "report card." Good communication can serve to rally the public to the president's side, but the ability to form congressional and interest group coalitions should not be overlooked either.

The Electoral Connection

One reason why presidents have trouble sustaining popularity is found in the difference between what it takes to win the presidency and what it takes to do the president's job. Winning the election involves assembling a winning coalition of voters in enough states to provide a majority vote in the electoral college. Candidates are often tempted to be vague on issues, to avoid alienating voters on either side. But a candidate who is too vague may appear wishy-washy. Once in office, a winning candidate may try to claim a mandate for his policies—claiming majoritarian backing from the voters. Divided government, with the presidency and Congress controlled by different parties, has made it more difficult in recent years for presidents to translate perceived mandates into policy, though polls suggest that the public prefers to have control of government divided between Democrats and Republicans, and scholars are divided in their assessment of the productivity of divided government.

The Executive Branch Establishment

The executive branch establishment gives a president substantial resources to translate an electoral mandate into public policy. He may call on the executive office of the president, the cabinet, or the vice president, or he may rely on his own staff, including his national security adviser, Council of Economic Advisers, and the Office of Management and Budget. The methods presidents use to organize their staffs differ from administration to administration and generally reflect the individual chief executive's own working style. Modern presidents usually rely much more heavily on the White House staff than on the cabinet (the heads of the executive departments and other officials) to make policy. Presidents Carter and Clinton are unusual in that each involved their respective vice president in substantive policy matters; in general, presidents have rarely looked to their vice presidents for assistance on such matters. In theory, the cabinet also acts as a presidential advisory group, but the importance of the cabinet has declined with the increase in the importance of the White House staff.

The President as National Leader

Presidents have differed considerably in their views of what government should do. Some, like Lyndon Johnson, emphasized the value of equality, while others, including Ronald Reagan, stressed freedom. The agendas they set grow out of their general political ideologies, tempered by the realities of political life in Washington. Those who enter office after serious upheavals or political crises may have great opportunities to reshape the political agenda. In the modern era, presidents have assumed significant leadership in the legislative process. Departments and agencies clear their budgets and proposed legislation through the president. Presidents also act as "chief lobbyists," trying to win support in Congress for their proposals. In this role, presidents may rely on their own personal contact with legislators, on contacts by their legislative liaison staffs, or on the aid of interest groups. Presidents may also use the threat of a veto as leverage to prevent Congress from passing measures of which they disapprove.

In addition to serving as national leader, a president is also the leader of his party. Yet, as President Clinton's experience with Fast Track demonstrated, close party ties do not always translate into policy success.

The President as World Leader

By virtue of America's position in the world , the president is not only a national leader, he is also a world leader. In that role, he must rely on his powers of persuasion; during periods of crisis, he needs good judgment and coolness under pressure. Even in the aftermath of the Cold War, presidents cannot ignore security issues, but they may find themselves paying more attention to the connection between foreign policy and domestic politics, especially where economic relations are concerned.

Presidential Character

In recent years, journalists have paid increasing attention to aspects of the "character issue." Scholars, too, have suggested that the electorate ought to pay more attention to a candidate's formative experiences and basic psychological makeup.

Key Terms

veto	mandate	Executive Office of the President
inherent powers	divided government	
		cabinet
delegation of powers	gridlock	
		legislative liaison staff

Research and Resources

For up-to-date printed information on the president's policies and actions, the best official source is the *Weekly Compilation of Presidential Documents* (Washington, D.C.: U.S. Government Printing Office), which is published every Monday by the Office of the Federal Register. For documents dating from 1993 on, you may wish to check on-line at <http://www.access.gpo.gov/nara/nara003.html>.

In addition to this resource, the Federal Register also issues an annual bound volume entitled *Public Papers of the Presidents of the United States* (Washington, D.C.: U.S. Government Printing Office). These volumes are useful for researching the presidency from Truman's administration to the present.

If you wish to study earlier occupants of the White House, you should turn to *A Compilation of the Messages and Papers of the Presidents, 1789–1927* (New York: Bureau of National Literature, 1928). This is a twenty-volume set containing official utterances of presidents from Washington to Coolidge.

These volumes include presidential proclamations, addresses, annual messages, veto messages, and other communications to Congress, as well as articles about the issues that faced each president.

For the interim period not covered by either of the two works above, you will find the following two privately published works useful:

Hoover, Herbert C. *The State Papers and Other Public Writings of Herbert Hoover*. Garden City, NY: Doubleday, Doran & Co., 1934.

Roosevelt, Franklin. *The Public Papers and Addresses of Franklin D. Roosevelt*. New York: Random House, 1938–1950.

Check the president's official Web site at www.whitehouse.gov for current information on the president.

For information on the Bush administration and cabinet, go to www.politics1.com. The site www.selectsmart.com allows you to see which presidential candidate most closely resembles your views.

For current information on-line, the White House maintains a Web site at <http://www.whitehouse.gov>. There you can read about the president and vice president, search presidential documents, check out current press releases, listen to speeches, and even tour the White House from your desktop. If you are interested in historical information on individual presidents, including sound and video clips, check out "Grolier Online's The American Presidency" at <http://www.grolier.com/presidents/>; also, see the Internet Public Library site at <http://www.ipl.org/ref/POTUS/> and Access Indiana's Guide to the Presidency at <http://tlc.ai.org/presindx.htm>. (This site contains a wide variety of links related to the occupants of the Oval Office.)

Using Your Knowledge

1. Using the resources suggested above, try to learn the president's position on the bill you researched in Chapter 10. Are there speeches or press conferences where he indicates his views on the bill? Is there a public ceremony where he delivered remarks as he signed the bill into law? Was there a veto message?

2. Use Gallup Poll or other survey data to construct a line graph showing the percentage of respondents who approve of the way President Reagan handled his job from 1981 to the end of his term. Do you observe any trends in your graph? How do the trends in your graph compare with the usual trend in presidential popularity sketched out in the text? Try the same exercise for Presidents Bush and Clinton.

3. Have you ever wanted to tell the president what you think? Pick up your phone and dial 1-202-456-1414, the White House telephone number. The electronic superhighway also runs through the White House. To send electronic mail to the president, use the following Internet address: <president@whitehouse.gov>. Of course, you are extremely unlikely to find the occupant of the Oval Office answering his own phone or responding to his own e-mail, but you can register your opinion on issues that are of significance to you. The White House does use this as one method of keeping track of public opinion.

Getting Involved

Ironically, perhaps, one accomplishment of the Clinton administration was the addition of the now-famous White House internship program. The program gives some 600 interns a year the opportunity to work in one of 22 White House offices, handling a range of chores from advance planning to staffing the visitors' office. Internships are available for twelve-week sessions in spring or fall or for six-week summer sessions. For further information, contact the White House Intern Program, Office of

The

Presidential Personnel, Old Executive Office Building, Room 151, Washington, D.C. 20500. Telephone: (202) 456-6676.

Sample Exam Questions

Multiple-Choice Questions

1. A president's power to persuade is
   a. specified in the Constitution.
   b. less important than his constitutional powers.
   c. often related to his popularity.
   d. not useful in distinguishing mediocre from above-average presidents.

2. Congressional delegation of power
   a. gives Congress more power to specify the details of policy.
   b. lets the executive have more latitude to implement policies.
   c. may not be rescinded without a two-thirds vote of both houses of Congress.
   d. has little impact on the balance of power between the executive and the legislature.

3. Lacking a mandate, President Bush emphasized national unity and bipartisanship instead of
   a. popular support.
   b. Republican support.
   c. Democratic support.
   d. NRA support.

4. The Constitution empowers the president to act in all of the following ways *except* as
   a. administrative head of the Union.
   b. chief of his political party.
   c. commander-in-chief of the military.
   d. treaty maker.

5. When President Lincoln blockaded Southern ports, he claimed the authority to do so based on
   a. the inherent powers of the presidency.
   b. a congressional delegation of power.
   c. executive privilege.
   d. the War Powers Resolution.

6. When government is unable to act on policy issues, the situation is described as
   a. a congressional mandate.
   b. a presidential mandate.
   c. gridlock.
   d. downsizing.

7. Article II of the Constitution explicitly gives the president the power to
   a. appoint and remove Supreme Court justices.
   b. veto legislation on a line-by-line basis.
   c. convene Congress.
   d. do all of the above.

8. The Constitution gives the power to act as commander-in-chief of the military to
   a. the Congress.
   b. the president, with the advice and consent of the Senate.
   c. the president.
   d. the president, on the advice of the National Security Council.

9. When a president claims that the voters have given him a special endorsement of his policies in an election, he is claiming
   a. inherent powers.
   b. a mandate.
   c. a congressional delegation of power.
   d. veto power.

10. Which of the following has *not* been a major factor in increasing presidential power?
    a. Constitutional amendments expanding presidential power
    b. The theory of inherent presidential power
    c. Crises such as war or depression
    d. Congressional delegations of power

11. Compared to prime ministers in western European democracies, American presidents
    a. have experience running executive departments at the national level.
    b. gain office by depending on their own campaign skills rather than party ties.
    c. have much experience in the national legislature.
    d. spend years working their way through the ranks in the party's hierarchy.

12. In recent times, most presidents have relied *most* heavily for advice on which of the following?
    a. The vice president
    b. The White House staff
    c. The cabinet
    d. The Senate

13. Which of the following is supported by data on presidential public appearances?
    a. With the introduction of radio and television, presidents have increased their reliance on the media, and public appearances have declined.
    b. Until the Nixon years, presidents made most of their public appearances in Washington, D.C.
    c. Democrats are more likely to make public appearances than are Republicans.
    d. None of the above.

14. The president's power to recognize other nations is
    a. derived from his power to receive ambassadors.
    b. subject to the advice and consent of the Senate.
    c. delegated by Congress.
    d. enumerated in Article II.

15. In attempting to translate his political vision into new legislation, a president may
    a. count on a "honeymoon" effect through his first term.
    b. use the line-item veto to reject parts of bills that do not fit in with his philosophy.
    c. use liaison staff and interest groups to pressure Congress.
    d. not involve himself in the legislative process once his bills are introduced.

16. According to Richard Neustadt, the key presidential power is
    a. the veto power.
    b. the power of the purse.
    c. the power to persuade.
    d. the appointment power.

17. During a president's first year in office, his program may stand a better chance of passage. This is due to the
    a. nature of divided government.
    b. fact that one house of Congress will be controlled by the president's party.
    c. fact that both houses of Congress will be controlled by the president's party.
    d. "honeymoon" effect.

18. The situation in which one party controls Congress while the other party controls the White House is known as
    a. the separation of powers.
    b. checks and balances.
    c. pluralism.
    d. divided government.

19. As originally ratified, the Constitution included which of the following among its requirements for presidential candidates?
    a. A natural born citizen who has lived in the United States for at least 14 years
    b. A male at least 35 years of age
    c. A white male at least 35 years of age
    d. A property owner

20. According to the text, one defense of presidential concern with popularity is that it
    a. may lead to government that is more responsive to the majority.
    b. may lead to government that is more responsive to special interests.
    c. results in more principled leadership.
    d. promotes equality.

21. The contemporary role of the president in the legislative process is *best* described as one in which
    a. the president proposes and Congress disposes.
    b. under the separation of powers, the president distances himself from the process.
    c. the president may serve as chief lobbyist and be active in all stages of legislation.
    d. the president is active only if his party controls Congress.

22. The major communications link between the president and Congress is the
    a. legislative liaison staff.
    b. vice president.
    c. cabinet.
    d. Office of Management and Budget.

23. Which of the following is *not* a part of the White House executive establishment?
    a. The Council of Economic Advisers
    b. The National Security Council
    c. The Office of Management and Budget
    d. The Executive Office of the President

24. During his time in office, President Clinton faced a number of difficult decisions involving the role of the United States and conflict abroad. Perhaps none was more agonizing than the fight in
    a. the Gulf.
    b. Kosovo.
    c. Haiti.
    d. Somalia.

25. Modern presidents are *less* likely to rely on their cabinet to make policy because
     a. the cabinet is too large and unwieldy to be a good policymaking body.
     b. cabinet members have limited areas of expertise. The secretary of agriculture may know very little about housing policy, for example.
     c. presidents have large White House staffs to take on this advisory role.
     d. of all of the above.

Essay Questions

1. Does divided government mean gridlock? Draw on research discussed in the chapter in formulating your answer.

2. What is the popular image of the presidency? How has this image created an impossible task for occupants of the Oval Office?

3. Explain the devices presidents have used to extend their power in areas where they were not given power by the Constitution.

4. Discuss the factors that help make presidents persuasive.

5. Do you think President Bush will have difficulty in passing his legislative preferences? What kind of resources can he use to gain support for his programs?

CHAPTER 13
The Bureaucracy

Learning Objectives

After reading this chapter you should be able to

- Define the key terms at the end of the chapter.
- List key factors that have contributed to the growth of the American bureaucracy.
- Explain the difficulties that surround efforts to reduce the size of the bureaucracy.
- Outline the basic types of organizations that make up the bureaucracy.
- Explain why presidents often feel they have inadequate control of the bureaucracy.
- Describe the formal and informal processes of bureaucratic policymaking.
- Explain the "rational comprehensive" model of decision making and compare it with real-world decision making.
- Give the main reasons why policies fail at the implementation stage.

The Bureaucracy and the Challenge of Democracy

The case of the ValuJet plane crash illustrates the dilemma created by Americans' rejecting big government but wanting the services big government provides. Every day, through the bureaucracy, the government is involved in hundreds of situations that involve conflicts among the values of freedom, order, and equality. Departments, bureaus, and agencies are required to make rules, to adjudicate, and to exercise administrative discretion to fill in the details left out of legislation passed by Congress. In their effort to achieve legislative goals, do bureaucrats go too far? Does the bureaucracy try to do too much? Is it out of control and out of touch?

From a majoritarian standpoint, the answers to these questions would seem to be yes. In recent years, the public has shown a preference for a smaller bureaucracy. Once again, however, we see the impact of pluralism on the American system. The various bureaus, agencies, and departments exist to do what some part of the population (call it a faction or an interest group) wants government to do. Often, the bureaucracy balances competing interests, thus doing a job political scientists think is essential if pluralism is to be democratic.

Efforts to reform the bureaucracy may run into trouble because of pluralist politics. Interest groups that have built up contacts with existing agencies will fight reorganization. Deregulation offers another method of reducing the bureaucracy, but it raises anew the fundamental question of values: It may provide greater freedom, but it may also result in inadequate protection, thus undermining order.

Chapter Overview

Organization Matters

The large, complex mass of organizations that administer the nation's laws and implement government policy is known as the bureaucracy. Although there is no one best way to structure all bureaucracies, it is clear that a bureaucracy's organization directly affects its ability to perform effectively.

Development of the Bureaucratic State

Government at all levels has grown enormously in the twentieth century. This growth results from several factors:

- Increased complexity, which changed society's attitudes about government's role in the marketplace
- Changed attitudes about government's social welfare responsibilities
- Ambitious officials who wish to expand their organizations to serve their clients more fully

On the whole, the public has little confidence in the government, but cuts in the government's size are difficult, since each part of the bureaucracy does a job some part of society wants done. Interest groups with a stake in an agency or department will often organize to resist cuts.

Bureaus and Bureaucrats

The bureaucracy is not a unified entity but a collection of dozens of government organizations, including the following:

- Fourteen departments—cabinet-level organizations that cover broad areas of government responsibility and contain within them numerous subsidiary offices and bureaus
- Independent agencies and regulatory commissions—not part of any cabinet department and controlled to varying degrees by the president
- Government corporations—organizations that provide services, such as mail delivery and passenger rail, that could be provided by the private sector but have been made public because Congress decided it better serves the public interest

The 2.8 million workers in the federal bureaucracy are part of the civil service, a system established to fill government jobs on the basis of merit rather than political patronage. The overall composition of the federal bureaucracy generally mirrors the population, although higher-level policymaking positions tend to be dominated by white males.

Among the members of the bureaucracy, ninety-nine percent are protected from party politics by civil service status; the remaining 1 percent is filled by people who are appointed by the president. Although presidential appointees fill the top policymaking jobs, the bulk of civil service employees are independent of the chief executive. Therefore, presidents often feel that they are unable to exert control over the bureaucracy and use it to achieve their purposes. In recent years, the national government has succeeded in reducing the number of bureaucrats without reducing government programs by transferring the jobs to private contractors, who are not considered government employees.

Administrative Policymaking: The Formal Processes

Congress gives the cabinet-level departments and agencies it creates administrative discretion—that is, authority to make policy within certain guidelines. Sometimes the guidelines are vague. The wide latitude Congress gives the bureaucracy sometimes leads to charges that the government is out of control. But Congress does have the power to review the legislation that establishes bureaucratic organizations. It also controls the purse strings. Informal contacts between members of Congress and agency personnel also help Congress communicate its intentions to the bureaucracy.

Administrative discretion is exercised through rule making—the quasi-legislative process of formulating and issuing regulations. Regulations have the force of law. They are created in accordance with a formal procedure that allows affected parties to register their views. Regulations serve to balance the needs of society The regulation-writing agency (such as the FDA) may attempt to strike a compromise between interests, but frequently compromises fail to please either side.

Administrative Policymaking: Informal Politics

Real-world decision making in government does not really resemble the textbook "rational-comprehensive" model, in which administrators rank their objectives and carefully weigh the costs and benefits of all possible solutions to a problem. In practice, policymakers find that their values often conflict—that their time, information, and options are limited, and the decisions that are best in theory may in reality be politically impracticable. Policymaking becomes a matter of "muddling through" and tends to be incremental, with policies changing only very gradually over time.

Bureaucracies develop written rules and regulations to promote efficiency and fairness. In addition, certain unwritten rules and norms evolve, influencing the way people act on the job. Employees in a bureaucracy—the bureaucrats—wish to advance their careers, and as a result they may avoid rocking the boat—that is, engaging in behavior that might violate written or unwritten canons.

Problems in Implementing Policy

Policies do not always do what they are designed to do. To find out why, it is necessary to look beyond the process of policymaking, to policy implementation. Policies may fail because the directives concerning them or their implementation may be vague or because lower-level officials have too much discretion. Programs may fail because of the complexity of government: the necessary coordination among federal agencies or among federal, state, and local agencies may be impossible to achieve. Policies may also fail because policymakers underestimate the capacity of an agency to carry them out. While bureaucrats have often been criticized for having too much discretion, more recently critics have charged that bureaucrats need more flexibility to be able to tailor their solutions to fit the specific context.

Reforming the Bureaucracy: More Control or Less?

Because organization makes a difference in a bureaucracy's ability to achieve its goals, people in government often tinker with organizational designs to make bureaucracy more effective. To ensure accountability in bureaucracy, Congress passed the Government Performance and Results Act, which requires each agency to develop strategic plans describing overall goals, objectives, and performance plans. The law required that beginning in 2000, all agencies must publish reports with performance data on each measure.

During the 2000 presidential election campaign, neither George Bush nor Al Gore talked much about reforming bureaucracy. They instead focused on new programs like prescription drugs for senior citizens.

Key Terms

bureaucracy	regulatory commission	rule making
bureaucrat	government corporation	regulations
department	civil service	incrementalism
independent agency	administrative discretion	norms

implementation   deregulation   Government Performance and Results Act

regulation   total quality management (TQM)

Research and Resources

The U.S. government bureaucracy is large and complex, but there are some good reference tools to help you make sense of it. The *United* States *Government Manual*, published annually and billed as the official handbook of the federal government, contains detailed information on all three branches of government as well as extensive material on departments and agencies. Typically, a description of an agency provides a list of its principal officials, a summary of its purposes and role in the government, an outline of its legislative or executive functions, and a description of its activities. In the back, the manual offers organizational charts of the agencies it describes. It is now available on the Internet in searchable form at <http://www.access.gpo.gov/nara/nara00l.html>. For help in finding federal regulatory information online, you might begin with "Introduction to Federal Regulatory Information" on the Internet at <http://asa.ugl.lib.umich.edu/chdocs/federalregs/intro.html>. For links to home pages of individual federal departments and agencies, check out this Library of Congress site: <http://lcweb.loc.gov/glolbal/executive/fed.html>.

Congressional Quarterly's Federal Regulatory Directory, 8th ed. (Washington, D.C.: Congressional Quarterly Press, 1996) contains much of the same information found in the *United States Government Manual*, though this work is not updated as frequently. It does have some other useful features, however. It opens with an introductory essay on the regulatory process, exploring the history of regulation and current trends and issues. It contains detailed profiles on major regulatory agencies, including analyses of their past histories, current issues, and future prospects. There are also brief biographical sketches of major administrators within each agency.

Using Your Knowledge

1. Using the *Federal Regulatory Directory* and the *United States Government Manual*, prepare a profile of at least two government departments. Outline the functions, present status, and future prospects of each. How large are their budgets? How many persons does each employ? Have these figures increased or decreased? Have its responsibilities grown or decreased recently?

2. Visit the Web sites for the agencies you profiled in question 1. Describe the information presented. Note the similarities and differences between the sites. What types of users would each site serve best?

Getting Involved

As the chapter noted, the national government employs people all over the country in virtually every field imaginable. If you are interested in government, you may want to consider a career working in one of the many departments, bureaus, or agencies of the federal system. As we noted in the text, all federal government employees (except for a very few political employees at the highest levels) are part of the civil service merit system. What should you do if you are interested in joining their ranks?

In the past, the Office of Personnel Management played the biggest role in the hiring process, but now the process is more decentralized. This means that in addition to visiting the Federal Job Information Center in your area and filling out Standard Form 171 (SF 171), the basic résumé form required in order to apply for most federal jobs, you'll also want to contact particular agencies where you think your talents and interests could be put to use. If you are interested in positions in the area of international affairs, be sure to look at the Getting Involved section in Chapter 20.

There are many useful resources to help you learn more about the federal job-seeking process. Here are two:

Krannich, Ronald, and Caryl Krannich. *Find a Federal Job Fast! Cutting the Red Tape of Getting Hired.* 4th ed. Woodbridge, VA: Impact Publications, 1998.

Pitz, Mary Elizabeth. *Careers in Government.* Lincolnwood, IL: VGM Career Horizons, 1995.

Be warned: despite the title of the Krannich and Krannich book, getting a government job is not always a quick process.

Sample Exam Questions

Multiple-Choice Questions

1. The management reform program known as TQM emphasizes
   a. treating citizens as customers.
   b. paying attention to environmental groups.
   c. paying attention to business interests.
   d. going by the book.

2. The way a bureaucracy is organized
   a. reflects its own survival needs.
   b. reflects the needs of its clients.
   c. affects its ability to accomplish its tasks.
   d. does all of the above.

3. The practice of filling government jobs with political allies or cronies is called
   a. total quality management.
   b. incrementalism.
   c. patronage.
   d. affirmative action.

4. The largest units of the executive branch, whose heads are members of the president's cabinet, are called
   a. departments.
   b. bureaus.
   c. regulatory commissions.
   d. independent agencies.

5. Regulatory commissions
   a. are totally immune to political pressure.
   b. may be indirectly influenced by presidents through their appointment power.
   c. may not be lobbied by interest groups.
   d. include Amtrak and the U.S. Postal Service.

6. The federal bureaucracy is made up of a workforce that
   a. is hired under a patronage system.
   b. works mainly in Washington, D.C.
   c. outside the highest levels, generally mirrors the population.
   d. over-represents women and minorities in policymaking positions.

7. The civil service fills jobs based on
   a. merit selection criteria.
   b. ideological agreement with the administration.
   c. patronage.
   d. political party affiliation.

8. The latitude Congress gives agencies to make policy consistent with their organizational missions is called
   a. administrative discretion.
   b. patronage.
   c. analytical budgeting.
   d. implementation.

9. The formal administrative procedure that results in the issuance of regulations is called
   a. adjudication.
   b. rule making.
   c. reorganization.
   d. implementation.

10. In recent years, the national government has succeeded in reducing the number of bureaucrats by
    a. turning over the jobs to private contractors.
    b. laying off employees.
    c. reducing government programs.
    d. doing none of the above.

11. Federal regulations are often
    a. made in a closed and secretive process.
    b. the result of an agency's attempt to balance competing interests.
    c. written in plain English to make them easily comprehensible.
    d. less effective than laws.

12. The informal, unwritten rules of behavior that develop in bureaucracies are called
    a. regulations.
    b. norms.
    c. esprit de corps.
    d. administrative discretion.

13. Real-world administrative decisions are made in a process *best* described
    a. by the "rational-comprehensive" model.
    b. as incremental or "muddling through."
    c. as immune from political pressure.
    d. as rooted in cost-benefit analysis.

14. According to the text, policies sometimes fail at the implementation stage because
    a. policy directives are unclear.
    b. coordination among implementing agencies is weak.
    c. policymakers have unrealistic expectations about an agency's capabilities.
    d. of all of the above.

15. When policies change slowly, bit by bit, step by step, over time, policymaking is said to be characterized by
    a. a planning-programming budgeting system.
    b. total quality management.
    c. management by objective.
    d. incrementalism.

16. The civil service was created after the assassination of
    a. James Garfield.
    b. Abraham Lincoln.
    c. Martin Luther King.
    d. John Kennedy.

17. Departments, agencies, and corporations receive their official mandates from
    a. Congress.
    b. the president.
    c. the Constitution.
    d. their clients.

18. In comparison with citizens in western European democracies, Americans spend a
    a. higher percentage of GNP and receive roughly the same benefits and services.
    b. higher percentage of GNP and receive more benefits and services.
    c. lower percentage of GNP and receive roughly the same benefits and services.
    d. lower percentage of GNP and receive fewer benefits and services.

19. According to the text, all of the following spurred the growth of bureaucracy *except*
    a. scientific and technological change.
    b. the desire to regulate business.
    c. the decline of the belief in progress.
    d. the belief that government should play a role in social welfare programs.

20. The main objective of the civil-service merit system was to reduce
    a. patronage.
    b. competence.
    c. decentralization.
    d. pork barrel politics.

21. Recent research on the U.S. Forest Service suggests that
    a. it has a long and successful history as an equal opportunity employer.
    b. women should not be hired in certain jobs.
    c. there are no differences between the attitudes of men and women in the Forest Service.
    d. hiring more women may result in a Forest Service that is more attuned to environmental protection.

22. The rational-comprehensive model is criticized as unrealistic because it overlooks the fact that
    a. policymakers have difficulty defining goals and agreeing on their priorities.
    b. the policies that are the best possible means to an end may not be politically palatable.
    c. policymakers act with incomplete information under time pressure.
    d. all of the above are true.

23. A new major initiative that holds agencies accountable for their performance is the
    a. Pendleton Act.
    b. Government Performance and Results Act.
    c. Reinventing Government Act.
    d. Smith Act.

24. Which of the following is an example of an independent agency?
    a. The National Endowment for the Arts
    b. The Office of Management and Budget
    c. The U.S. Postal Service
    d. The Federal Communication Commission

25. According to pollsters, which of the following options is *most* popular for dealing with the anticipated budget surplus?
    a. Increase defense spending on military salaries and high-tech weapons.
    b. Increase domestic spending on Social Security, Medicare, and education.
    c. Reduce the national debt.
    d. Cut taxes.

Essay Questions

1. Why was the civil service system introduced? Why is the system often frustrating to presidents?

2. What are the key problems associated with administrative discretion?

3. What does it mean to act "bureaucratically"? How do "by-the-book" bureaucrats actually advance democratic values?

4. Why is it so difficult to control bureaucrats?

5. Outline and explain the factors that have contributed to the growth of the bureaucracy.

CHAPTER 14
The Courts

Learning Objectives

After reading this chapter you should be able to

- Define the key terms at the end of the chapter.
- Explain the concept of judicial review and how it was established in *Marbury v. Madison.*
- Sketch the basic organization of the federal court system.
- Explain the role of the federal district courts and federal appeals courts.
- Describe two ways in which judges exercise a policymaking role.
- Outline the routes by which cases come to the Supreme Court.
- Describe the formal procedures at the Supreme Court's biweekly conferences.
- Explain ways in which justices, particularly the chief justice, influence court decisions.
- Describe the process of appointment to the federal judiciary.
- Evaluate the Supreme Court as an instrument of pluralist or majoritarian democracy.

The Courts and the Challenge of Democracy

In the American system, the courts interpret the law. Courts are made up of judges, and judges bring their own value systems with them to the job. Each judge will give a different weight to freedom, order, and equality. Since federal judges hold lifetime appointments to insulate them from politics, a president's judicial appointees will continue to make decisions long after he leaves office. They may do so without regard for the will of the majority. The decision of the Supreme Court in the 2000 election overturned the ruling of the Florida Court and set aside a constitutional crisis, raising the question of partisanship on the part of the Supreme Court.

When judges interpret laws and precedents loosely in ways that are heavily influenced by their own values, they are said to be judicial activists. When they stick closely to the letter of the law and let their own preferences intrude as little as possible, they are said to exercise judicial restraint. Is judicial activism compatible with democracy? Sometimes it has promoted democratic ends—as in the "one person, one vote" decisions, for example. But the judiciary itself is the least democratic branch of government. Its members are protected from popular control. They are appointed, not elected, and they serve life terms. Through judicial review, the Supreme Court may, and has, overruled acts of the popularly elected Congress. These attributes of the judiciary may seem undemocratic. The power of the Supreme Court in the 2000 presidential election posed a problem for democratic theory, which is based on the right of the people to determine their elected officials.

Chapter Overview

In American democracy, the court system is involved in many decisions. Yet, the courts themselves are largely beyond democratic control. Judges are limited by statutes and precedents, but they still have substantial leeway in deciding how to interpret them. Thus their own values often influence their interpretations, setting the stage for judicial restraint or judicial activism.

National Judicial Supremacy

The founders could not agree on the details concerning the structure of the federal judiciary. So after creating a single, supreme court, they left most of the details up to the First Congress. By the Judiciary Act of 1789, Congress established a system made up of district courts, circuit courts, and the Supreme Court.

Under Chief Justice John Marshall, the Supreme Court developed into a powerful branch of government that could check the power of other branches through its use of judicial review. In *Marbury v. Madison*, the Court for the first time declared a congressional statute unconstitutional. The Court thus established itself as the final authority on the meaning of the Constitution.

The Organization of the Courts

The American court system is complex. In addition to a national system, there are separate court systems operating in each state. The main entry points for cases into the national judicial system are the 94 federal district courts, which hear criminal cases involving violations of federal law, civil cases brought under federal law and in which the federal government is the plaintiff or defendant, and civil cases between citizens of different states when more than $75,000 is at issue.

Federal courts handle far fewer cases than do state courts, but the number of cases in federal courts has grown and is generally related to the overall level of social, political, and economic activity in the nation.

Judges exert a policymaking function by applying rules (precedents) established in prior decisions (common or "judge-made" law) and by interpreting legislative acts (through a process of "statutory construction").

Appeals may be carried from federal district courts to one of the 13 courts of appeals. Judges in the appeals courts sit in panels of three. They write and publish opinions on the cases they hear. These opinions establish legal precedents that serve as a basis for continuity and stability, following the principle of *stare decisis*.

Since relatively few cases are ever actually brought to the Supreme Court, the decision of a lower court is usually the final word. The decentralization of the system allows for individual judges in various district or circuit courts to interpret laws differently; this lack of uniformity may cause difficulties until, eventually, discrepancies are resolved by a Supreme Court decision.

The Supreme Court

The Supreme Court makes national policies—its decisions affect the nation as a whole. The Court's caseload includes a few cases that it hears as part of its original jurisdiction under the Constitution, but the main body of cases comes to the Court on appeal from lower courts or state courts.

The Court controls its docket and hears very few cases. Cases usually come to it only after all other avenues have been exhausted. Cases must also involve a substantial federal question. At least four justices must agree to hear a case, or it is not argued before the Court.

In deciding which cases to review, the Court often takes cues from the solicitor general, the Department of Justice official who represents the government before the Court. The solicitor general performs a dual role as an advocate for the president's policy preferences and as an officer of the Court, defending the institutional interests of the federal government.

After a case has been heard, the nine judges meet in conference to discuss their positions. A formal vote decides the outcome. As they approach cases, justices may differ in their view of their role. Some may practice judicial restraint, trying to stick closely to the intent of the legislators who made the law and to previous decisions of the courts. Other justices may take on the role of judicial activist, interpreting the law more loosely and in accord with their own policy preferences. In recent history, as a result of many activist judges' support for liberal ideas, judicial activism has been associated with liberalism. But the decision in the case of *Bush v. Gore* proves that conservative judges can also become judicial activists.

Although justices may agree on what the particular result of a case should be, they may not agree fully on the legal reason for the decision. In the Supreme Court's policymaking, both the Court's decision and the reasons offered for it are important. The opinion, or explanation of reasons for a decision, is critical. Sometimes justices may shift their votes if they do not believe an opinion is based on legal reasoning they are able to support.

Justices will try to win the support of their fellow justices in conference and also through their opinion writing. They may also try to influence the selection of personnel for the Court.

The chief justice is particularly well placed to exercise leadership on the Court. He or she directs the conference and by tradition speaks first and votes last in court deliberations. When voting with the majority, the chief justice assigns the opinion. Astute use of these powers can make the chief justice an intellectual leader, a social leader, and a policy leader, although perhaps only Chief Justice Marshall ever fully filled all three roles.

Judicial Recruitment

There are no formal constitutional requirements for federal judgeships, though a set of standards has evolved. By law, judges must be approved by the Senate. Over the years, an informal practice known as "senatorial courtesy" has given the senior senator of the president's party a substantial amount of control over judicial appointments in his state, although this power is not as extensive as it once was. In addition, the American Bar Association screens candidates and ranks them as qualified or unqualified for office, though it has recently lost its officially sanctioned role in the appointment process.

Presidents generally seek to appoint judges who share their ideological orientation. Thus, while President Carter sought judges who mirrored the population in race and gender, Presidents Reagan and Bush looked for judges who valued order and appointed fewer women and minorities to the federal bench. President Clinton, like President Carter, sought greater diversity in his appointments.

The Consequences of Judicial Decisions

Only a small percentage of federal cases wind up in court. Many civil cases end in out-of-court settlements. In criminal cases, defendant often admit guilt and plea bargain.

Although the courts have the power to make judgments, they do not have the power to implement the policies they make. They must rely on the other branches of government for that. Judicial opinions are not always popular. Courts as institutions may appear to be countermajoritarian. Yet, a study of Supreme Court decisions shows that the Court mirrored public opinion in more than 60 percent of its decisions. (Two major exceptions are the abortion issue, where the public is sharply divided, and school prayer, where the public opposes the Court's decisions.) Key reasons for this are that the Court tends to defer to the law, and the law tends to mirror public opinion. Despite the controversy over the decision in the election of 2000, the Gallup Poll showed no erosion of public confidence in the Supreme Court.

The Courts and Models of Democracy

The major question in evaluating the role of the courts as creators of policy concerns how far judges stray from existing statutes and precedents. Majoritarians would want judges to cling closely to the letter of the law, leaving it to the elected legislature to decide how much emphasis to put on equality or order. Pluralists think the values of judges should come into play to advance the values and interests of the population. Several aspects of the judicial system make it conform to the pluralist model. Among these are the decentralized court system, which offers multiple access points to the legal system, and class action suits, which allow individuals to pool their claims.

Key Terms

judicial review	criminal case	civil case

common (judge-made) law	federal question	judgment
U.S. district courts	docket	argument
U.S. courts of appeals	rule of four	concurrence
precedent	solicitor general	dissent
stare decisis	*amicus curiae* brief	senatorial courtesy
original jurisdiction	judicial restraint	plea bargain
appellate jurisdiction	judicial activism	class action

Research and Resources

An excellent starting point for research on the Supreme Court is *Congressional Quarterly's Guide to the U.S. Supreme Court*, 3rd ed. (Washington, D.C.: Congressional Quarterly Press, 1996). This hefty volume contains a brief (sixty-page) overview of the origins and development of the Court and detailed analyses of the role of the Court in the federal system, of Court decisions on individual rights, of pressures on the Court, and of the Court at work. It includes brief biographies of every justice who ever served on the Court and short summaries of major decisions.

What if you need more than a brief summary of a case—what if you must examine the actual opinion handed down by the Court? Suppose, for example, that you wanted to find the Supreme Court decision that forced President Nixon to surrender the Watergate tapes. The Internet really simplifies the task. One method would be to use "Findlaw: Internet Legal Resources" at <http://www.findlaw.com/>. Not only does this site provide information about law schools and a wide array of legal subjects, it also provides the text of Supreme Court and Circuit Court opinions (back to 1893) and allows you to search using the names of the parties to the case, the citation of the case, or words found in the text of the opinion. At the "Oyez" site, <http://court.it-services.nwu.edu/oyez/>, you locate cases by selecting from a number of keywords. At "Selected Historic Cases of the Supreme Court," <http://supct. law.cornell.edu/supct/ cases/historic.htm>, you can search a selected data base of historic cases using an even wider variety of topics. If you are not able to use the Internet, consult the subject index in the back of *Guenther's United States Supreme Court Decisions*. Look up the word *Watergate* and you will find a reference leading to the place where the case you want appears in the listing in the front of the book. Regardless of the source you use, you will find the case cited as *United States v. Richard M. Nixon*, 418 US 683. This citation for the case refers to where it appears in *U.S. Reports*, the official version of the opinion published by the U.S. Government Printing Office. The number preceding "US" indicates the volume number, while the number following "US" gives the page number where the case is to be found.

Sometimes, if you are working on a project that involves references to eighteenth- and nineteenth-century cases, you will find cases cited in this way:

Calder v. Bull (3 Dall. 386), 1798.

Fletcher v. Peck (6 Cr. 87), 1810.

McCulloch v. Maryland (4 Wheat. 316), 1819.

Until 1875, the official reports of the Supreme Court were designated by the last name of the court reporter who recorded the decisions. The abbreviations in the above examples stand for the first three court reporters, whose names were Dallas, Cranch, and Wheaton. The citation for the *McCulloch* case tells you that it will be found in the fourth volume of Wheaton's reports, on page 316.

Here is a list of the early reporters, their dates, and the redesignations assigned to make each conform to the *U.S. Reports* system:

Early Designation		Abbr.	Dates Covered	U.S. Reports
1–4	Dallas	(Dall.)	(1790–1800)	1–4
1–9	Cranch	(Cr.)	(1801–1815)	5–13
1–12	Wheaton	(Wheat.)	(1816–1827)	14–25
1–24	Howard	(How.)	(1843–1860)	42–65
1–2	Black	(Black)	(1861–1862)	66–67
1–23	Wallace	(Wall.)	(1863–1874)	68–90

To cite a case in a footnote or bibliography, you should include the official name of the case (usually the names of the two parties to the case), the volume of the report where the case appears (for example, Cr., Wall., U.S.), the page number where the decision may be found, and the year in which the case was decided.

Other Judicial Sites. In addition to providing access to cases, the "Oyez" mentioned above offers an opportunity to listen to the actual oral arguments of a large selection of cases before the Supreme Court, as well as extensive biographical material on the justices and a virtual tour of the Court building. The Federal Judicial Homepage, <http://www.uscourts.gov>, offers general information about the court system as well as a map showing the circuits at <http://www.uscourts.gov/links.html>. The American Judicature Society, which promotes the effective administration of justice and includes judges and lawyers as well as lay people in its membership, can be found on-line at <http://www.ajs.org/>.

Using Your Knowledge

1. Using the procedures outlined in the Research and Resources section above, locate the following cases:

    *   the *VMI* case
    *   cases involving *Hustler* publisher, Larry Flynt
    *   *Roe v. Wade*

    Find each opinion on-line or on the library shelf, and copy the citation from each opinion.

2. Using the resources outlined in the section above, prepare a list of Supreme Court decisions dealing with each of these subjects:

    *   executive privilege
    *   children's rights
    *   the Internet
    *   the veto power

    Give a full citation for each case.

3. Listen to the oral argument for at least one of the cases you find in question 1 or 2 above.

Getting Involved

If you see yourself sitting on the Supreme Court some day, perhaps you would like to take a crack at an internship while you are still in college. Most opportunities to work at the Supreme Court take the form of clerkships and are available only to recent law school graduates. There are, however, a small number of highly competitive internships available to undergraduates. Some background in constitutional law is usually expected. Internships are available in summer, fall, and winter. They are unpaid, although a small scholarship may be available. For further information, contact the Supreme Court of the United States,

Judicial Internship Program, Office of the Administrative Assistant to the Chief Justice, Room 5, Washington, D.C. 20543. Telephone: (202) 479-3374.

The American Judicature Society offers unpaid internships for undergraduate and graduate students interested in the administration of justice, the improvement of the courts, and law and society issues. Interns have earned academic credit for their experiences. More details are available at <http://www. ajs.org/internl.htm1>. Contact: Seth Andersen, Program Manager/Internship Coordinator, American Judicature Society, 180 N. Michigan Ave., Suite 600, Chicago, IL 60601. Telephone: (312) 558-6900, ext. 105. E-mail: <sandersen@ajs.org>.

Sample Exam Questions

Multiple-Choice Questions

1. When judges interject their own values into their interpretation of cases, they are said to practice
   a. liberalism.
   b. conservatism.
   c. judicial restraint.
   d. judicial activism.

2. The power to declare congressional acts invalid is called
   a. judicial review.
   b. judicial restraint.
   c. judicial activism.
   d. adjudication.

3. Judicial review of congressional legislation was first established in the case of
   a. *Marbury v. Madison.*
   b. *Fletcher v. Peck.*
   c. *McCulloch v. Maryland.*
   d. *Barron v. Baltimore.*

4. The Constitution created
   a. only the Supreme Court and established its original jurisdiction.
   b. only the Supreme Court and established its appellate jurisdiction.
   c. only the Supreme Court and established its size.
   d. the Supreme Court as well as the circuit courts of appeals and the district courts.

5. Federal district courts
   a. are the trial courts in the federal system.
   b. usually publish written opinions.
   c. hear all civil cases between citizens of different states.
   d. are the appeals court in the federal system.

6. Congress may change all of the following *except*
   a. the organization of district and circuit courts.
   b. the Supreme Court's appellate jurisdiction.
   c. the Supreme Court's original jurisdiction.
   d. the number of justices on the Supreme Court.

7. U.S. circuit courts
   a. are the main trial courts of the system.
   b. are appellate courts.
   c. rarely issue written opinions.
   d. do not establish precedents.

8. The expression for the bias in favor of precedents or existing decisions is
    a. *stare decisis.*
    b. tort.
    c. *amicus curiae.*
    d. judicial review.

9. When a justice supports a judgment but disagrees with other justices on the reasons for deciding that way, he or she may write a separate opinion called a
    a. dissenting opinion.
    b. concurring opinion.
    c. writ of certiorari.
    d. unanimous opinion.

10. The official who represents the government before the Supreme Court is called the
    a. solicitor general.
    b. public defender.
    c. attorney general.
    d. *amicus curiae.*

11. In general, the chief justice
    a. assigns all opinions.
    b. assigns opinions when voting with the majority.
    c. speaks last in conference.
    d. votes first in conference.

12. Which of the following *best* describes the current role of the American Bar Association in the judicial appointment process?
    a. By statute, all appointees must receive an ABA rating of "well-qualified" to be eligible for a judicial appointment.
    b. It is currently prohibited from screening candidates.
    c. By custom, it ranks candidates, and its rankings are always followed.
    d. It no longer plays an officially sanctioned role.

13. By overturning the Florida Court and delivering a victory for the Republicans, the majority of the Supreme Court judges can be called
    a. liberal judicial activists.
    b. liberal judicial restrainists.
    c. conservative judicial activists.
    d. conservative judicial restrainists.

14. Any future confirmations of Supreme Court judges will be as ____ as any confirmation contest in recent memory.
    a. easy
    b. intense
    c. compromised
    d. latent

15. To win Senate confirmation, judicial nominees usually need
    a. to be political neutrals.
    b. to have support from the state's senior senator in the president's party.
    c. to promise to practice judicial restraint.
    d. to do all of the above.

16. The Gallup Poll taken after the 2000 election found
    a. an erosion in public confidence in the Supreme Court.
    b. no erosion in confidence in the Supreme Court.
    c. that a majority of Americans distrust the Supreme Court.
    d. none of the above.

17. Most criminal cases
    a. end up in federal courts.
    b. wind up in the Supreme Court.
    c. end up by plea bargaining.
    d. are taken to trial.

18. In flag-burning cases, the Supreme Court affirmed the value of
    a. order.
    b. freedom.
    c. equality.
    d. majoritarianism.

19. For a state case to come before the Supreme Court,
    a. appeals in the state court system must be exhausted.
    b. it must raise a federal question.
    c. it must receive a writ of certiorari.
    d. all of the above must occur.

20. Supreme Court decisions
    a. embody the principles of majoritarian government.
    b. are consistently out of step with public opinion.
    c. mirror public opinion on abortion and school prayer.
    d. are surprisingly consistent with public opinion.

21. The doctrine of national supremacy requires that the Supreme Court
    a. be the final interpreter of both national and state laws.
    b. be the final interpreter of national laws only.
    c. be the final interpreter of state laws only.
    d. subordinate the Constitution to states' rights.

22. Which of the following is *not* a component of judicial review established in *Marbury v. Madison*?
    a. Courts may declare federal, state, or local laws invalid.
    b. Federal laws and treaties take precedence over state or local laws when there is a conflict.
    c. The Supreme Court is the final authority on the meaning of the Constitution.
    d. State courts are obliged to follow the Constitution only as it is interpreted by state courts.

23. Federal judges have life tenure and protected salaries in order to make them
    a. responsible to the majority of the people.
    b. responsible to the legislature that confirmed them.
    c. responsible to the executive who appointed them.
    d. independent.

24. Taken as a whole, the judicial appointments of which of the following presidents were *least* representative of the distribution of the population on race and gender?
    a. Ronald Reagan
    b. George Bush
    c. Jimmy Carter
    d. Bill Clinton

25. Maintaining public order through criminal law is mainly a function of the
    a. national government.
    b. national and state governments.
    c. state governments.
    d. state and local governments.

Essay Questions

1. Distinguish between judicial restraint and judicial activism. Is there a necessary connection between restraint and activism on the one hand and political ideology on the other?

2. What is "judicial review"? Explain how it was established in *Marbury v. Madison*.

3. What are the main differences between federal district courts and U.S. circuit courts?

4. How can a chief justice exert leadership on the Supreme Court? Give concrete examples to illustrate your answer.

5. How do judicial recruitments under Presidents Carter, Reagan, Bush, and Clinton compare?

CHAPTER 15
Order and Civil Liberties

Learning Objectives

After reading this chapter you should able to

- Define the key terms at the end of the chapter.
- Distinguish between civil rights and civil liberties.
- Explain how the establishment clause of the First Amendment has been interpreted in cases involving government aid to church-related schools, prayer in public schools, and nativity displays on public property.
- Show how the free-exercise clause of the First Amendment has been applied to the issues of compulsory saluting of the flag and the use of drugs as a sacrament.
- Describe the two approaches developed by the Supreme Court for dealing with cases involving the free-expression clause of the First Amendment.
- Outline the evolution of the clear and present danger test.
- List the major exceptions to the First Amendment's protection of freedom of speech.
- Discuss prior restraint, libel, and censorship as possible limitations on freedom of the press in America.
- Explain how the Fourteenth Amendment has been used to extend the protections of the Bill of Rights to citizens in cases involving the states.
- Explain where the Supreme Court found the right to privacy in the Constitution, and show how this right has been applied in cases involving abortion, birth control, and homosexuality.

Order and Civil Liberties and the Challenge of Democracy

The availability of cyberspace changes the way we communicate; and, in the bargain, it presents many new conflicts of values. This chapter looks at how the courts have resolved conflicts among the three values that are so important to democratic politics—order, freedom, and equality. Court decisions involve a balancing act among these values. A review of the cases in the chapter may lead a person to conclude that not one of these values is ever preferred unconditionally over the others. The freedoms of speech, press, and assembly are all particularly important to the conduct of democracy, yet the Supreme Court has sometimes limited them in the name of order when exercising these freedoms would create a very serious danger. Furthermore, where certain types of expression are concerned—for example, obscenity—the Court may choose to uphold the value of order by supporting community standards. On the other hand, the fact that the exercise of these freedoms may offer an affront to the majority and threaten to disrupt established patterns of social order is not always enough to convince the Court to restrict them.

Courts may forbid prayer in public schools under any circumstances, but they may sometimes find that public monies can be used to fund nativity displays or aid church schools. The courts balance freedom and order in these instances.

As a part of the task of upholding order, the government punishes those who violate laws and endanger the lives and property of others. Yet, those accused of crimes may not be deprived of their freedoms without due process of law. This means, among other things, that they must be informed of their legal rights, including the right to an attorney and to protection against self-incrimination. Enforcing these rights may sometimes mean that guilty people go free, but in balancing order and freedom, the courts often decide that the threat to order posed by freeing a guilty person is less worrisome than the threat to freedom that is posed by denying an accused person due process of law.

With respect to the right to personal autonomy, the Supreme Court has given mixed signals. In cases involving abortion and contraception, the Court has defended individual freedom. But in *Bowers v. Hardwick*, the Court rejected the value of individual freedom and supported the right of states to preserve social order by outlawing homosexual acts.

The Court often uses the Bill of Rights to protect citizens from the national government. But the Bill of Rights did not initially apply to the states; so while the national government was barred, for example, from using illegally obtained evidence in trials, state courts were not. Gradually in this century, however, the Court has used the Fourteenth Amendment to extend the provisions of the Bill of Rights to the states as well.

Chapter Overview

The Bill of Rights

In the American system, the values of freedom, equality, and order often conflict. In such cases, each side may claim that its view is rooted in the law. Disputes over issues involving such basic values are usually settled in the courts by our unelected judiciary. Conflicts often arise from different views on the rights of citizens, and a major source of people's rights is the Constitution—in the Bill of Rights and the Fourteenth Amendment. The Constitution guarantees civil rights and civil liberties. A civil right declares what the government must do or provide; a civil liberty is a guarantee to individual citizens that acts as a restraint on government.

Freedom of Religion

The First Amendment provides for freedom of religion, speech, press, and assembly. These protections of individual freedoms may conflict with the need for order—an example of the original dilemma of government discussed in Chapter 1. Freedom of religion is guaranteed in two clauses. The first, the establishment clause, forbids any law that would create an official religion; the second, the free-exercise clause, prevents the government from interfering with the practice of religion. The establishment clause erected "a wall of separation between church and state." The government is also supposed to be neutral between religions and between the religious and the nonreligious. On certain issues, such as government aid to church-related schools and government-funded nativity displays, the Supreme Court has allowed what opponents have seen as violations of the establishment clause. Reasoning that textbook loans and transportation are aids to students, not churches, the Court has allowed some support to church schools. In 1971, the *Lemon* test put forth guidelines for determining constitutionality under the establishment clause. Arguing that nativity scenes surrounded by secular symbols of the Christmas season aided in the celebration of a national holiday and had only indirect, remote, and incidental benefits to religion, the Court allowed public funding of the displays. The Court loosened its application of the *Lemon* test by allowing public school teachers to provide government-mandated classes to disadvantaged youngsters in New York parochial schools. On the issue of school prayer, however, the Court has maintained a consistent position that public school prayer violates the establishment clause. In 2000, the Supreme Court struck down the practice of organized student-led prayer at public high school football games.

The free-exercise clause also gives rise to conflicts when the practice of a certain religion leads a person to do what is forbidden by law or to refuse to do what is required by law. A person may not be forced to take a job that requires him or her to work on the Sabbath, but the Court has forbidden participation in traditional religious rituals that involve the use of illegal drugs. The Court reasoned that religious beliefs are inviolate, but antisocial actions in the name of religion are not protected by the Constitution. The perceived narrowing of the range of free expression of religion led Congress to pass the Religious Freedom Restoration Act which required the government to meet strict scrutiny before interfering with religious practices. The Court quickly ruled the popular act unconstitutional, noting that Congress could not change the Constitution.

Freedom of Expression

Freedom of expression, including freedom of speech and freedom of the press, provides a right to unrestricted discussion of public affairs, yet these rights have never been absolute. Initially, the First Amendment clauses seemed aimed at preventing prior restraint. As the First Amendment speech doctrines developed, justices argued that speech creating a "clear and present danger" may be limited. "Symbolic speech" and "fighting words" may receive even less protection, though the Supreme Court has ruled that flag burning is a constitutionally protected form of expression. Obscenity—although hard to define—is not protected by the Constitution, and the Court agreed that the government can regulate distribution of obscene materials. Yet, the Court has also affirmed broad latitude for freedom of speech in cyberspace. In 1999, a federal court issued a permanent injunction closing a Web site of some anti-abortion advocates who threatened doctors performing abortions.

Freedom of the press, including the ability to collect and report information without government interference, is crucial in a free society. Print media defend this freedom as absolute, although electronic media have had to accept some government regulation. Individuals may sue the media for libel, but public figures must show that there is actual malice involved when publishers print false statements about them. Basically, freedom of the press means freedom from prior restraint. The Court has been reluctant to limit freedom of the press in order to ensure a fair trial. Yet, reporters are not protected from the demands of law enforcement and may be required to reveal their sources. Only in the most extreme and compelling cases has prior restraint been considered justified, as, for example, when publishing certain material might mean nuclear annihilation.

The First Amendment also provides the right to peaceably assemble and to petition the government for redress of grievances. This right has merged with freedom of speech and freedom of the press under the general heading of freedom of expression.

The Right to Bear Arms

The Second Amendment's guarantee of the right to keep and bear arms is a source of great controversy. Advocates of gun control see the guarantee as a collective one, centered on the right of states to maintain militias. Opponents of gun control argue that the amendment protects the individual's right to own guns.

Applying the Bill of Rights to the States

The Bill of Rights was created to put limits on the power of the national government. Initially, its provisions did not apply to states. Under the Fourteenth Amendment, however, nearly all of the Bill of Rights have gradually been extended to all levels of government. The Fourteenth Amendment guarantees people due process of law. The Court has interpreted this provision to mean that, in criminal proceedings, defendants in both state and national cases must be told about their constitutional rights, including their right to remain silent and their right to an attorney. The Court still allows jury size in trials to vary from state to state, however. The right to an attorney is considered fundamental, while the right to trial by a jury of a certain size is not. In one of the important cases of 2000, the court reaffirmed that *Miranda* had a constitutional rule, which Congress could not undermine through legislation. The Fourth Amendment provides people with freedom from unreasonable searches and seizures. The exclusionary rule, which disallows the use of evidence obtained illegally, helps to ensure this right, though this rule has been weakened in recent years. Interpretation of the exclusionary rule continues to divide the Court and serves as an example of the conflict between freedom and order.

The Ninth Amendment and Personal Autonomy

The Ninth Amendment left open the possibility that there were other rights, not enumerated, that might also be free from government interference. In the 1960s and 1970s, the Supreme Court used the Ninth Amendment as the basis for asserting that people have a right to privacy and that that right allows individuals to make their own choices about birth control and abortion. The appointment of conservative justices under Presidents Reagan and Bush placed gay rights and abortion rights in question, but President Clinton's appointees seem more likely to support these unenumerated rights.

Constitutionalizing Public Policies

The discovery of new rights under the Ninth Amendment creates a difficulty for democracy. It removes questions about value conflicts from the arena of democratic politics and puts them under the protection of the Constitution and the unelected judicial branch.

Key Terms and Cases

Terms

civil liberties	free-expression clauses	ex post facto law
civil rights establishment clause	clear and present danger test	obligation of contracts
free-exercise clause	fighting words	*Miranda* warning
strict scrutiny	public figures	exclusionary rule
prior restraint	bill of attainder	good faith exception

Cases

Lemon v. Kurtzman	*New York Times v. Sullivan*
Sherbert v. Verner	*New York Times v. United States*
Brandenburg v. Ohio	*Palko v. Connecticut*
Tinker v. Des Moines Independent County School District	*Gideon v. Wainwright*
	Griswold v. Connecticut
Cohen v. California	*Roe v. Wade*
Miller v. California	
	Bowers v. Hardwick

Research and Resources

This chapter deals mostly with the protection and extension of civil liberties as a result of Supreme Court decisions. The text describes the Court's recent discovery of a right to privacy. In the 1970s, Congress also took some measures to protect two individual rights not explicitly specified in the Constitution, namely the right to privacy and the right to information. Congress passed a pair of acts known as the Privacy Act and the Freedom of Information Act. The first of these grants all individuals access to information the government keeps about them; the second gives people a right to see much of the information collected by the government. This section of the study guide outlines methods for using these acts.

If you have used government documents, you have no doubt been amazed by the range of subjects they cover. Published government documents are only the tip of the information iceberg. The government collects information on practically everything, and much of that material is in file drawers and computers in Washington rather than publicly disseminated in the form of published government documents.

How do you get information that is gathered, but not published, by the government? What rights do you have to it?

Answers to these questions are found in the Freedom of Information Act (FOIA). The FOIA, first passed in 1966, marked a revolution in government record handling. The act shifted the burden of proof. Formerly, the person requesting information had been required to convince the government that the material should be provided; now the government must provide information unless it can give a specific reason under the statute why the information should be denied. One Food and Drug Administration official reported that as a result of the FOIA his agency "went from a situation in which about l0 percent of our records were disclosed before the act to a situation where now we estimate about 90 percent of the categories of records we have are disclosed."

The FOIA applies to information held by the administrative agencies of the government (including the executive office of the president), but it does not apply to records held by Congress, the courts, or state governments (virtually every state has its own act governing availability of public records). In 1974, the FOIA was amended, speeding and easing the process of gaining access to records.

What sort of information may come to light under the FOIA? Here are some examples:

- FBI reports on high-profile deceased individuals at <http://www.fbi.gov/foipa/foipa.htm>
- Records of regulatory agencies concerning pollution control programs (Environmental Protection Agency)
- Government files on UFOs (FBI)
- Consumer complaints registered with the Fair Trade Commission

Under statute, nine categories of information may be denied you, including agency personnel records; material on criminal investigations that might be an invasion of personal privacy, deprive a person of the right to a fair trial, or compromise a confidential source; and properly classified national defense or foreign policy secrets. For information on how to file an FOIA request, see the Web site of the Society of Professional Journalists at <http://www.spj.org/foia/index.htm> or try this ACLU site at <http://www.aclu.org/library/foia.html>.

The FOIA protects your access to government materials, but under its provisions, you may be denied information of a sensitive or personal nature about individuals. You do have a right to obtain personal information about yourself, however. Under the Privacy Act, if you are an American citizen, you are entitled to access government records kept about you. The government will have records on you in the following instances:

- You have ever applied for a federal grant or loan, including student aid.
- You have ever worked for a federal agency or government contractor or were a member of the armed forces.
- You were ever arrested by your local police and fingerprinted and the FBI has a record of the arrest.
- You have ever traveled abroad and the Department of State has a file on your conduct abroad.
- You have ever received Medicare or social security benefits.

To obtain information under the Privacy Act, follow the procedures sketched out by the FOIA. You can adapt the model to reflect the fact that you are using the provisions of the Privacy Act of 1974, 5 U.S.C. 522a.

For printed information on these two laws, see *A Citizen's Guide on Using the Freedom of Information Act and the Privacy Act of 1974 to Request Government Records*, published by the Government Printing Office.

Using Your Knowledge

1. Follow the process sketched out in the Research and Resources section to prepare a request for information obtainable under the Freedom of Information Act or the Privacy Act.

2. Visit the FBI's electronic reading room, and browse the files for well-known people such as Mickey Mantle, Elvis Presley, John Wayne, and Jackie Robinson. What kinds of information were collected?

Sample Exam Questions

Multiple-Choice Questions

1. The Bill of Rights was proposed
    a. as a means of eliminating opposition to the Constitution.
    b. by antifederalists as a means of scuttling the Constitution.
    c. as an integral part of the Constitution.
    d. as a necessary limit on the power of state governments.

2. The establishment clause of the First Amendment
    a. establishes the United States as a Christian nation.
    b. forbids the establishment of an official religion.
    c. has been used by the Supreme Court to justify the practice of prayer in public schools.
    d. has outlawed any government funding for education in church schools.

3. The three-pronged test to determine whether aid to church schools is constitutional is called the
    a. *Lemon* test.
    b. Miranda test.
    c. clear and present danger test.
    d. Engle test.

4. The Religious Freedom Restoration Act was struck down by the Supreme Court because
    a. the Bill of Rights does not apply to the states.
    b. the city of Boerne did not have standing to sue.
    c. Congress passed it by a narrow margin.
    d. it amounted to an amendment of the First Amendment, and Congress alone cannot amend the constitution.

5. The Supreme Court's rulings on school prayer
    a. are a triumph for majoritarian politics.
    b. underscore the pluralist nature of American democracy.
    c. may be overridden by an act of Congress.
    d. offer no protection for minority rights.

6. The free-exercise clause of the First Amendment
   a. permits all beliefs and practices of all religions.
   b. permits all beliefs but allows for limitation of antisocial religious practices.
   c. may, in rare cases, allow the government to compel belief.
   d. protects beliefs and practices of Christianity only.

7. The press clause has been *most* effective in prohibiting
   a. prior restraint on publications.
   b. libel suits for works published.
   c. requirements that news reporters reveal their sources.
   d. regulation of obscene publications.

8. Under the First Amendment, freedom of speech
   a. is absolute.
   b. extends equally to verbal and symbolic or nonverbal expression.
   c. may be limited when a speech is designed to provoke lawless action and has a high probability of doing so.
   d. is prohibited to communists or members of the Ku Klux Klan.

9. With regard to the Communications Decency Act, the Supreme Court
   a. struck it down as an unconstitutional abridgement of freedom of speech.
   b. struck it down because Internet pornography should be regulated by the states.
   c. upheld it because the Internet was more like TV than print and regulation of TV is permitted.
   d. upheld it because most of the justices are conservative and the act was favored by conservatives.

10. The right to keep and bear arms
    a. is linked in the Constitution to the need for a well-regulated militia.
    b. entitles citizens to own any type of weapon.
    c. may not be subject to state or federal licensing restrictions.
    d. All of the above are true.

11. In *U.S. v. Eichman*, the Supreme Court
    a. struck down a constitutional provision against flag burning.
    b. upheld a constitutional provision against flag burning.
    c. struck down a federal law against flag burning.
    d. upheld a federal law against flag burning.

12. The protections of the Bill of Rights have gradually been extended to the states through
    a. the Fourteenth Amendment.
    b. the *Slaughterhouse* cases.
    c. *Barron v. Baltimore*.
    d. the privileges and immunities clause.

13. The Sixth Amendment provision for a right to counsel was extended to the states in
    a. *Palko v. Connecticut*.
    b. *Near v. Minnesota*.
    c. *Gideon v. Wainwright*.
    d. *Miranda v. Arizona*.

14. The *Miranda* warning
    a. protects against illegal search and seizure.
    b. informs suspects of their right to remain silent and to be represented by an attorney.
    c. informs suspects of their right to a trial by a twelve-person jury.
    d. protects suspects against being placed in double jeopardy.

15. The main source used by the Supreme Court to justify introducing an unenumerated right of privacy was the
    a. Fourteenth Amendment.
    b. Ninth Amendment.
    c. Sixth Amendment.
    d. Second Amendment.

16. In *Roe v. Wade*, the Supreme Court
    a. upheld order over freedom.
    b. rejected all state regulation of abortion.
    c. left decisions on abortion up to a mother and her physician during the first three months of pregnancy.
    d. permanently settled the abortion question.

17. The United States has endorsed the gist of the Council of Europe's Cyber-Crime Treaty, which aims to harmonize laws against all of the following *except*
    a. hacking.
    b. Internet fraud.
    c. child pornography.
    d. libels.

18. Under current Supreme Court interpretations of the right to privacy, states must permit all of the following *except*
    a. unrestricted rights to abortion during the first trimester of pregnancy.
    b. use of birth-control devices.
    c. homosexual sodomy.
    d. abortions in the second trimester when the health of the mother has been protected.

19. The Defense of Marriage Act
    a. bans homosexual marriage throughout the United States.
    b. eliminates the "marriage penalty" or income taxes.
    c. permits a state to refuse to recognize a homosexual marriage sanctioned by another state.
    d. criminalizes homosexual practices between consenting adults.

20. Which of the following is prohibited *both* to national and state governments under the Constitution?
    a. Passing ex post facto laws
    b. Passing bills of attainder
    c. Impairing the obligation of contract
    d. All of the above

21. The clear and present danger test
    a. was originally enunciated by Justice Holmes in the *Gitlow* case.
    b. distinguishes the advocacy of ideas from the incitement to disorder.
    c. was first applied by Jefferson to the Alien and Sedition Acts.
    d. applies not only to speech but also to symbolic expression and matters of personal appearance.

22. In 2000, Justice O'Connor sided with a coalition of liberal and moderate justices in striking down
    a. *Roe v. Wade.*
    b. the *Lemon* test.
    c. partial birth abortion.
    d. the right to counsel.

23. Cases involving the exclusionary rule on the seizure of evidence raise a conflict between
    a. freedom and order.
    b. freedom and equality.
    c. equality and order.
    d. none of the above.

24. If high school students wished to meet on school property in an after school study group, they would be
    a. permitted to meet under the Equal Access Act.
    b. denied access because of Supreme Court rulings based on the establishment clause.
    c. denied access because prayer in the schools is unconstitutional.
    d. permitted to meet only if students from all other religions also organized groups.

25. Before the Fourteenth Amendment was passed and applied to the states, the Constitution still barred both state and national governments from
    a. passing ex post facto laws.
    b. establishing an official religion.
    c. denying citizens the right to a jury trial.
    d. searching property without warrants.

Essay Questions

1. What conflicts arise between the values of freedom, order, and equality when the government attempts to regulate pornography in cyberspace?

2. Where did the Supreme Court find the right to privacy? Outline activities in this area that are currently protected and those that are exempted from protection.

3. What is meant by "constitutionalizing public policy"? What dilemmas does this practice create for democracy? Give examples to illustrate your answer.

4. Trace the use of the due process clause as a means of making the protections of the Bill of Rights effective against the states.

5. In deciding cases involving civil liberties, has the Supreme Court held freedom, equality, or order as an absolute value? Defend your answer by providing examples from cases discussed in this chapter.

CHAPTER 16
Equality and Civil Rights

Learning Objectives

After reading this chapter you should be able to

- Define the key terms at the end of the chapter.
- Explain why the Civil War amendments proved ineffective in ensuring racial equality.
- Outline the NAACP's strategy for ending school segregation.
- Distinguish between *de jure* and *de facto* segregation.
- Describe the tactics of the civil rights movement and the passage of the 1964 Civil Rights Act.
- Show how protectionist legislation discriminated against women.
- List the major legislative and judicial milestones in the struggle for equal rights for women.
- Explain why women's rights advocates favored the Equal Rights Amendment (ERA) as a way to extend equal rights to women.
- Discuss how affirmative action programs have led to charges of reverse discrimination.
- Distinguish between equality of opportunity and equality of outcome.

Equality and Civil Rights and the Challenge of Democracy

Based on a 2000 U.S. State Department report, racial discrimination still persists in the United States. In the past, the advocates of social, political, and economic equality have relied on legal, moral, political, and spiritual authority to abolish racial discrimination. Under the new treaty, advocates of racial equality may appeal to an international authority to end racial or other forms of discrimination.

Over the past few decades, however, the government's priorities have shifted. With the separate-but-equal decision in *Plessy v. Ferguson* in 1876, the national government tried to sweep the conflict between equality and freedom under the rug. By announcing in *Brown v. Board of Education* in 1954 that "separate is inherently unequal," the national government faced the tension between freedom and equality and the fact that more of one usually means less of the other. The meaning of equality also creates difficulties. Many who agree on the need for equality of opportunity will not support measures they think are geared to produce equality of outcome.

The struggle for civil rights also illustrates the conflict between pluralism and majoritarianism. In accepting the demands of African American citizens, the national government acts in a way that is more pluralist than majoritarian. As Chapter 1 pointed out, majoritarian democracy does what the majority wants and thus may allow discrimination against minorities, even though the substantive outcome (inequality) seems undemocratic.

Thus, questions about what kind of public policies should be adopted to achieve equality are often highly controversial. If the nation wants to promote racial and gender equality among doctors or sheet-metal workers, for example, it may design policies to help previously disadvantaged and underrepresented groups gain jobs in these areas. This practice, however, may lead to charges of reverse discrimination.

African Americans seeking civil rights not only had to contend with being members of a minority group, they also were largely excluded from the electoral process. Under the leadership of the National Association for the Advancement of Colored People (NAACP), they adopted the strategies of lobbying legislators and pressing claims before the judiciary, the branch of government least susceptible to majoritarian influences. Later, as the civil rights movement grew (and as majority opinion became more hospitable to their cause), they emphasized the importance of legislation as a method of achieving equality and also used the techniques of civil disobedience to challenge laws they believed to be unjust.

The women's movement offers an interesting contrast. Women are not actually a minority group; they are a majority of the population. Yet, in the struggle to pass the Equal Rights Amendment (ERA), pluralism prevailed! Although a majority of Americans favored the amendment, it failed. The amending process, by requiring extraordinary majorities, gives enormous power to minorities bent on thwarting a particular cause.

Chapter Overview

Two Conceptions of Equality

Throughout much of American history, civil rights—the powers and privileges supposedly guaranteed to individuals and protected from arbitrary removal at the hand of government—have often been denied to certain citizens on the basis of their race or sex. The pursuit of civil rights in America has been a story of the search for social and economic equality. But people differ on what equality means. Most Americans support equal opportunity, but many are less committed to equality of outcome.

The Civil War Amendments

After the Civil War, the Thirteenth, Fourteen, and Fifteenth amendments were passed to ensure freedom and equality for African Americans. In addition, as a response to the black codes, Congress passed civil rights acts in 1866 and 1875 to guarantee civil rights and access to public accommodations. While the legislative branch was attempting to strengthen African American civil rights, the judicial branch seemed intent on weakening them through a number of decisions that gave states room to maneuver around civil rights laws. States responded with a variety of measures limiting the rights of African Americans, including poll taxes, grandfather clauses that prevented them from voting, and Jim Crow laws that restricted their use of public facilities. These restrictions were upheld in *Plessy v. Ferguson*, which justified them under the separate-but-equal doctrine. By the end of the nineteenth century, segregation was firmly and legally entrenched in the South.

The Dismantling of School Segregation

The NAACP led the campaign for African American civil rights. Its activists used the mechanism of the courts to press for equal facilities for African Americans and then to challenge the constitutionality of the separate-but-equal doctrine itself. In 1954, in *Brown v. Board of Education*, a class-action suit, the Supreme Court reversed its earlier decision in the *Plessy* case. It ruled that "separate educational facilities are inherently unequal" and that segregated schools must be integrated "with all deliberate speed" under the direction of the federal courts. The Court thus ordered an end to school segregation that had been imposed by law (*de jure* segregation), but in many parts of the country segregation persisted, because African Americans and whites lived in different areas and sent their children to local schools (*de facto* segregation). This problem led the courts to require the unpopular remedy of bussing African American and white children as a means of integrating schools. By 1974, however, the Supreme Court began to limit bussing as ordered by the judicial branch.

The Civil Rights Movement

The NAACP's use of the legal system ended school segregation and achieved some other, more limited, goals, but additional pressure for desegregation in all aspects of American life grew out of the civil rights movement. The first salvo in the civil rights movement came when African Americans in Montgomery, Alabama, boycotted the city's bus system to protest Rosa Parks' arrest and the law that prohibited African Americans from sitting in the front of buses. Under the leadership of Martin Luther King, Jr., the movement grew, and civil rights activities, including nonviolent civil disobedience, spread.

In the early 1960s, President Kennedy was gradually won over to supporting the civil rights movement. In 1963, he asked Congress to outlaw segregation in public accommodations. Following Kennedy's death, President Lyndon Johnson made passage of the Civil Rights Act of 1964 his top legislative priority, and the bill passed despite a long debate and filibuster in the Senate. More civil rights legislation followed in 1965 and 1968. This time, the legality of civil rights acts was upheld by the Supreme Court.

Having civil rights laws on the books does not mean discrimination will end once and for all, however. For one thing, the courts must interpret the laws and apply them to individual cases. In the Grove City College case, the Supreme Court offered a very narrow interpretation of a civil rights law, in effect taking the teeth out of the legislation. Congress reasserted its original, more sweeping intent in the Civil Rights Restoration Act of 1988.

Meanwhile, the Court, with a new conservative majority in the ascendancy, continued to issue decisions limiting the scope of previous civil rights rulings. Civil rights groups looked to Congress to restore rights previously recognized, but presidential vetoes scuttled such measures until 1991.

Despite Dr. King's commitment to nonviolence, the struggle for civil rights was not always a peaceful one. White violence against civil rights workers included murders and bombings. By the late 1960s, racial violence had increased as African Americans demanded their rights but many whites remained unwilling to recognize them. The African American nationalist movements, often militant, promoted "black power" and helped instill racial pride in African Americans.

Civil Rights for Other Minorities

Civil rights legislation won through the struggles of African Americans also protects other minorities. Native Americans, Latinos, and disabled Americans were also often victims of discrimination. Native Americans were not even considered citizens until 1924. The Indian reservations established by the U.S. government were poverty stricken. In the late 1960s and early 1970s, the frustrations of Native Americans erupted into militancy. By the mid-1970s and early 1980s, they began to win important legal victories, including compensation for land taken by the U.S. government. Recently, new entrepreneurial tribal leadership of Indian tribes has capitalized on the special status of their tribes and enjoyed economic success by sponsoring casino gambling ventures.

Latinos who migrated to the United States seeking economic opportunities found poverty and discrimination instead. This problem was compounded by the language barrier and the inattention of public officials to their needs. Latinos, too, have used the courts to gain greater representation on governing bodies. Recently, they have begun to be successful in obtaining elected and appointed political offices.

Building on the model of existing civil rights laws, disabled Americans managed to gain recognition as an oppressed minority and, through the 1990 Americans with Disabilities Act, receive the protection of a right of access to employment and facilities.

Homosexual Americans

Though gays and lesbians have made significant progress, they have not yet succeeded in passing a complete civil rights law protecting their rights. The 2000 Supreme Court decision in *Boy Scouts of America v. Dale* illustrated the continued struggles of gays and lesbians for civil rights.

Gender and Equal Rights: The Women's Movement

Civil rights have long been denied to women, partly as a result of policies designed to protect women from ill treatment. Only after a long struggle did women win the right to vote under the Nineteenth Amendment that was passed in 1920. But gaining the vote did not automatically bring equality for women. Discrimination continued in the workplace and elsewhere. It took legislation such as the 1963 Equal Pay Act, the 1964 Civil Rights Act, and Title IX of the Education Amendments Act of 1972 to prohibit some of the other forms of discrimination against women. In the early 1970s, the Court began to strike down gender-based discriminations that could not be justified as serving an important government purpose. In 1996, the Court applied a new standard of "skeptical scrutiny" to acts denying rights based on sex. This new standard makes distinctions based on sex almost as suspect as those based on race.

For many years, the Court proved reluctant to use the Fourteenth Amendment as the basis for guaranteeing women's rights. As a result, proponents of equal rights for women sought an amendment to ensure that women's rights stood on a clear constitutional footing. Although the ERA was ratified by 35 states, it fell three states short of the minimum required for adoption and did not become the law of the land, although many states eventually adopted their own ERAs. Some scholars argue that, in practice, the Supreme Court has since implemented the equivalent of the ERA through its decisions.

Affirmative Action: Equal Opportunity or Equal Outcome?

The Johnson administration started a number of programs to overcome the effects of past discrimination by extending opportunities to groups previously denied rights. These affirmative action programs involved positive or active steps taken to assist members of groups formerly denied equality of opportunity.

These programs soon led to charges of reverse discrimination. The Court, however, has found some role for affirmative action programs. In the *Bakke* decision, a split court held that race could be one of several constitutionally permissible admissions criteria. In other cases, the Court has allowed the use of quotas to correct past discriminatory practices. In the *Adarand* case, however, the Court decided that programs that award benefits based on race must themselves be held up to a strict scrutiny standard—a test few could pass. Based on the *Adarand* case, a federal court in 1996 rejected the use of race or ethnicity as a condition for admission to the University of Texas law school.

Key Terms and Cases

Terms

affirmative action	racism	*de facto* segregation
equality of opportunity	poll tax	civil rights movement
equality of outcome	racial segregation	boycott
invidious discrimination	separate-but-equal doctrine	civil disobedience
civil rights	desegregation	protectionism
black codes	*de jure* segregation	Nineteenth Amendment
sexism	Equal Rights Amendment (ERA)	

Cases

Plessy v. Ferguson

Brown v. Board of Education

Brown v. Board of Education II

United States v. Virginia

Regents of the University of California v. Bakke

Adarand Constructors v. Peña

Johnson v. Transportation Agency, Santa Clara County

Research and Resources

Chapter 14 in this guide explained how to find a Supreme Court opinion. Once you have located an opinion, however, you might still have some difficulty figuring out how to read it. Cases are reported beginning with a heading that gives the parties to the case, the docket number, the dates the argument was heard, and the date the decision was handed down. Next, in rather small print, comes the syllabus. This includes a summary of the facts of the case and the legal questions it raised, as well as a summary of what the Court decided, or held, in the case. Next comes a paragraph, also part of the syllabus, explaining how the justices divided on the opinion. This paragraph identifies (1) the author of the Court's opinion, (2) the justices who joined in that opinion, (3) those who concurred with it, and (4) those who dissented.

Justices *concur* when they vote with the majority on the actual decision but do not fully agree with the reasoning behind the majority's decision. Justices in this position often write separate opinions detailing their differences with the opinion of the Court and outlining the grounds on which they based their vote. Justices who are in the minority may choose to write dissenting opinions explaining the reasons for their disagreement with the majority. Writers of concurring and dissenting opinions all try to set out alternative views of the case, hoping that their views might influence and persuade Court members in future decisions.

After the syllabus comes the full text of the opinion of the Court. The opinion of the Court ends with the judgment—for example, "affirmed" or "denied." This is followed by the full text of any concurring opinions and then by any dissenting opinions.

More Civil Rights Web sites. Learn more about the NAACP, its role in the civil rights movement, and its current agenda by visiting its Web site at <http://www.naacp.org/>. Take a virtual tour of the National Civil Rights Museum at <http://www.mecca.org/~crights/>. The site features material on topics including *Brown v. Board of Education of Topeka*, the Montgomery Bus Boycott, and the March on Washington. Hear civil rights' leaders Martin Luther King and Malcolm X at <http://www.webcorp.com/civilrights/index.htm>.

The Human Rights Campaign lobbies for gay and lesbian rights. Visit their Web site at <http://www.hrcusa.org/>. The Feminist Majority Foundation's Web site has a wealth of information on women's rights in the United States and worldwide. Their URL is <http://www.feminist.org/>. For rights of the disabled, see The Disability Rights Activist Web site at <http://www.teleport.com/~abarhydt/index.html>.

Using Your Knowledge

1. Select three of the cases discussed in this chapter of the text. Look them up in *U.S. Reports,* or find them on-line. (See Chapter 14 of this guide.) For each case, note the vote tally, who authored the opinion of the Court, which justices joined in that opinion, which ones wrote concurring opinions, and which ones wrote dissents. Did any justices join in the concurring or dissenting opinions?

2. Visit the Web sites of at least two civil rights' groups. You may want to start with some of those listed above. Compare the key issues facing each group and the strategies they are using to deal with those issues.

Getting Involved

Students interested in civil rights work have internship opportunities available. Here are two examples.

The Latino Civil Rights Task Force works on behalf of Latinos in the Washington area. Unpaid semester-long internships as legal aides, media coordinators, or research assistants are available to seniors. For further information, contact Mr. Pedro Aviles, Executive Director, 1815 Adams Mill Road, Washington, D.C. 20009. Telephone: (202) 332-1053.

The NOW Legal Defense and Educational Fund has internships in New York and Washington for undergraduates interested in policy projects on women's rights. Contact Ms. Jackie Butler, Administrative Assistant, NOW Legal Defense and Educational Fund, 99 Hudson Street, New York, NY 10013. Check out NOW's home page at <http://www.now.org/now>.

Sample Exam Questions

Multiple-Choice Questions

1. The part of the Constitution that outlaws slavery is the
   a. Equal Rights Amendment.
   b. Thirteenth Amendment.
   c. Fourteenth Amendment.
   d. Fifteenth Amendment.

2. The Court struck down the public accommodations section of the Civil Rights Act of 1875 on the grounds that
   a. the national government could not interfere with states' rights to act in ways that discriminate.
   b. private acts of discrimination were beyond the government's reach.
   c. separate-but-equal facilities were provided for African Americans and whites.
   d. the Fourteenth Amendment did not apply to the states.

3. The Court decision that upheld separate-but-equal facilities for African Americans and whites was
   a. *Plessy v. Ferguson*.
   b. *Brown v. Board of Education*.
   c. *Sweatt v. Painter*.
   d. the *McLaurin* case.

4. All of the following resulted from the civil rights movement *except*
   a. increasing numbers of African Americans in public office.
   b. more African American voters.
   c. an immediate end to *de facto* and *de jure* segregation of schools.
   d. an increase in African American nationalism.

5. The principal tactics used by the NAACP in its struggle to dismantle school segregation included
   a. boycotting and sit-ins.
   b. lobbying and legal challenges.
   c. demonstrations and voter registration drives.
   d. rioting and violence.

6. School segregation that results from the racial patterns of neighborhood housing is called
   a. *de facto* segregation.
   b. *de jure* segregation.
   c. government-imposed segregation.
   d. separate-but-equal facilities.

7. Affirmative action
   a. emphasizes equality of opportunity more than equality of result.
   b. requires the establishment of strict quotas.
   c. is an effort to ameliorate the effects of invidious discrimination.
   d. does all of the above.

8. The 1964 Civil Rights Act
   a. protects only blacks.
   b. forbade employment discrimination against women.
   c. made relatively few changes to the status quo.
   d. was declared unconstitutional in *Heart of Atlanta Motel v. U.S.*

9. The failure of the Equal Rights Amendment was an example of
   a. the majoritarian theory of democracy.
   b. the power of committed minorities in a pluralist system.
   c. a rejection of minority rights.
   d. the triumph of equality over freedom.

10. The Voting Rights Act of 1965
    a. was declared unconstitutional.
    b. had little effect on African American registration, because of *de facto* segregation.
    c. is applied equally to all parts of the country.
    d. aims at improving voter registration among minority groups.

11. American public opinion on affirmative action
    a. is strongly negative.
    b. is strongly positive.
    c. is evenly divided.
    d. varies considerably, depending on the wording of the question.

12. The law that prohibited sex discrimination in federally aided education programs was
    a. the Elementary and Secondary Education Act of 1965.
    b. the Civil Rights Act of 1964.
    c. the Education Amendments Act of 1972.
    d. the Equal Rights Amendment.

13. The Court's ruling in *Grove City College v. Bell*
    a. broadly interpreted Title IX of the Education Amendments Act of 1972.
    b. was the target of the Civil Rights Restoration Act of 1988.
    c. was accepted by Congress as a faithful interpretation of legislative intent.
    d. applied the law to entire institutions whenever any part of them discriminates against women or minorities.

14. The Greensboro lunch counter sit-ins were examples of
    a. nonviolent civil disobedience.
    b. unconstitutional actions on the part of demonstrators.
    c. tactics disapproved of by Martin Luther King, Jr.
    d. an ineffective tactic used only in that locality.

15. The separate-but-equal doctrine was first overturned by the Supreme Court in
    a. *Brown v. Board of Education.*
    b. *Sweatt v. Painter.*
    c. *Milliken v. Bradley.*
    d. *Grove City College v. Bell.*

16. The reason the U.S. Department of State is charged with implementing racial discrimination is
    a. multiculturalism.
    b. diversity.
    c. globalism.
    d. localism.

17. A catalog of racial abuses includes all of the following *except*
    a. inadequate enforcement of existing anti-discrimination laws.
    b. persistent discrimination in employment.
    c. continued segregation in housing.
    d. segregation in the military.

18. The poll tax was
    a. outlawed by the Twenty-Fourth Amendment.
    b. outlawed by the Thirteenth Amendment.
    c. declared unconstitutional in the *Grove City College* case.
    d. imposed only on African Americans.

19. The commitment by employers, schools, or other institutions to expand opportunities for women, African Americans, Latinos, and other minorities
    a. is called affirmative action.
    b. was declared unconstitutional by the Supreme Court in 1987.
    c. pits order against freedom.
    d. All of the above are true.

20. All of the following advanced the equality of women *except*
    a. the Nineteenth Amendment.
    b. protective legislation.
    c. the Equal Pay Act of 1963.
    d. the Civil Rights Act of 1964.

21. Which of the following was *not* a method used to keep African Americans from voting?
    a. Poll taxes
    b. Literacy tests
    c. Grandfather clauses
    d. Separate-but-equal elections

22. Supreme Court Justice Blackmun asserted that in order to get beyond racism, we must take account of
    a. race.
    b. segregation.
    c. reverse discrimination.
    d. affirmative action.

23. The percentage systems have been introduced to replace affirmative action in all of the following states *except*
    a. California.
    b. Texas.
    c. Florida.
    d. Arkansas.

24. The *Boy Scouts v. Dale* decision illustrates both the continuing legal struggles of gays and lesbians for civil rights and modern conflict between
    a. pluralism and majoritarianism.
    b. freedom and equality.
    c. the majority and minorities.
    d. liberty and fair trials.

25. The Civil Rights Act of 1964 did all of the following *except*
    a. provide that federal funds could be withheld from programs that discriminate.
    b. provide for bussing to end *de jure* segregation.
    c. prohibit racial discrimination in public accommodations.
    d. outlaw job discrimination based on sex.

Essay Questions

1. Explain the responsibility of the State Department to enforce anti-discrimination laws. What problems would it encounter in enforcing such laws?

2. What major methods of political participation did the NAACP use in the effort to integrate schools and by the civil rights movement in the effort to secure passage of civil rights legislation?

3. How was "protective" legislation a form of discrimination against women?

4. Explain what is meant by affirmative action. Is affirmative action a kind of reverse discrimination? How did the Supreme Court rule in the *Bakke* case?

5. Distinguish between "equality of opportunity" and "equality of outcome." Which is more controversial? Why?

CHAPTER 17
Policymaking

Learning Objectives

After reading this chapter you should be able to

- Define the key terms at the end of the chapter.
- Sketch four categories for analyzing public policy.
- Describe the four main stages in the policymaking process.
- Explain the causes of the fragmentation that often occurs in policymaking in America.
- Describe the means used to achieve coordination of policies.
- Explain the dynamics of issue network politics.
- Point out the differences between "iron triangles," "issue networks," and "nonprofit organizations."
- List the advantages and disadvantages of relying on "in-and-outers" to shape public policy.
- Outline the advantages and disadvantages of policy subsystems in a democracy.

Policymaking and the Challenge of Democracy

The government seeks to achieve its purposes by adopting plans of action, or policies. Government has several different, often competing purposes, including maintaining order, promoting freedom, and enhancing equality. Different people inside and outside government attach different weights to these purposes, in general and often in specific cases as well. Given the multiplicity of actors, values, and interests involved in the political process, policymaking can be a complicated, sometimes contradictory business, where plans often have unintended results.

Policymaking in the American system can be highly fragmented. Different organs of the national government often have overlapping jurisdictions or areas of responsibility. State governments, too, may develop policies. This fragmentation makes the policymaking process conform to the pluralist model. We have seen that the general public is not very well informed about politics; a weakness of the majoritarian model is that it threatens us with government by people who have little knowledge behind their decisions. In contrast, the people who make up issue networks concerned with specific areas of public policy bring enormous expertise to bear in public policy matters. Their activities fit well with a pluralist model of democracy, which promises considerable influence in the policy process to those with the greatest stake in an issue area. However, if pluralist politics is to be democratic, access must be open, and different interests must be able to compete on a relatively equal basis.

Chapter Overview

Government Purposes and Public Policies

Governments attempt to achieve their purposes through public policies—that is, plans of action they adopt to solve social problems, counter threats, or use opportunities. Public policies are the means by which governments pursue certain goals in specific situations. Because people disagree on their perceptions of situations and on the appropriateness of goals and means, they differ on which public policies should be adopted.

To analyze public policies, it helps to divide them up into four categories—policies that prohibit, policies that protect, policies that promote, and policies that provide. Governments prohibit when they outlaw certain behavior: murder or drug taking, for example. They protect through regulations limiting damage that might be inflicted on a protected group of people, things, or activities. They promote activities by using incentives to encourage people to engage in the activities. The tax structure is a frequent source of incentives made available through "tax expenditures"—that is, revenue that the government does not collect in taxes in order to stimulate the activity the government wants to promote. Last, governments provide benefits to people. Benefits may be collective (like roads or schools) or selective (like student loans, flood insurance, or food stamps).

The Policymaking Process

Different kinds of policies affect the political process in different ways. Some policies pit well-organized groups against each other. The American system of pluralism often leads to compromises among competing groups. Sometimes competing groups may try to advance their interests by supporting different types of policies than their competitors.

Most policymaking processes include the following four stages:

- An agenda-setting stage, in which a problem is defined as a political problem
- A policy-formulation stage, in which possible solutions are developed in the form of policy proposals and decisions are made about which proposal (if any) to adopt
- An implementation stage, in which a policy is carried out (often amid difficulties in coordinating the activities of government officials at various levels, who must implement the policy)
- A policy-evaluation stage, in which programs are analyzed to discover how well they work in practice.

Evaluation results in feedback—that is, information that lets policymakers know how well programs are doing what they were created to do and whether they should be continued, expanded, changed, or cut. Feedback may lead to new items being put on the political agenda and, hence, to a new cycle of policymaking.

A Multiplicity of Participants

The fundamental nature of American government—federalism and the separation of powers—contributes to the fragmentation of policymaking by creating multiple centers of power. These centers of power may pursue competing policies in the same policy area. This circumstance may be the result of real conflict between branches of government or merely a lack of coordination within a branch. Sometimes, problems of fragmentation and coordination may be attacked by reassignment of agency jurisdictions, by reform of congressional committees, by Office of Management and Budget regulatory review, or by industry appeals for a single national policy to replace 50 state policies in an issue area.

The Nonprofit Sector

Community-based organizations have become important players in the policymaking process. Nonprofits are voluntary organizations that use government funds to implement a government program. They provide vitally important services. According to one scholar, they are "the glue that holds civil society together."

Issue Networks

In any given issue area, many interest groups try to influence policy. These private sector actors are effective when they are able to provide technical mastery of a policy area. In Washington, American government often amounts to "government by policy area," which involves interaction among various governmental institutions and private sector organizations. When changes in the Clean Air Act were considered, for example, a group of actors emerged with shared knowledge of this aspect of environmental policy, including members of Congress, EPA bureaucrats, consultants, lawyers representing environmentalists, lawyers representing industries, and trade associations represented by public relations firms trying to sway public opinion. These actors, who share a knowledge of and an interest in the particular policy under consideration, form an issue network.

In the past, political scientists often described policy areas as being dominated by subgovernments, or "iron triangles"—tightly knit subsystems made up of the congressional committee leaders, key agency and bureau personnel, and top lobbyists concerned with a particular issue. More recently, the concept of "issue networks" has emerged to describe the policymaking process. Issue networks include a large and varied group of participants and are more easily penetrated than iron triangles (although they are still held together by technical mastery of particular policy areas).

Policy Expertise

Individuals in an issue network speak the same language; they are united by shared knowledge of and experience in a policy area. The expertise of private sector participants is often acquired by working in government before switching to the private sector. In Washington, where access and influence are crucial to success, "in-and-outers" build up both the knowledge and the connections that enable them to be heard and to earn lucrative rewards for their services. This creates certain ethical dilemmas, including the possibility of conflicts of interest. The 1978 Ethics in Government Act was passed to limit quick-and-easy movement between government jobs and the private sector. More recently, the Clinton administration adopted some new rules to limit lobbying by people recently employed in top government jobs, but these rules have proved ineffective.

Issue Networks and Democracy

Though issue networks are more open than iron triangles, both fail to achieve the majoritarian vision of democratic government. Although it is desirable to have those with expertise influence policymaking, the dominance of iron triangles and issue networks in the process may make policymaking appear too responsive to the demands of small groups and hence undemocratic.

Key Terms

public policy	implementation	nonprofit organization
agenda setting	policy evaluation	issue network
issue definition	feedback	in-and-outer
policy formulation	fragmentation	

Research and Resources

Who makes up issue networks and iron triangles? Who influences policymaking? What are their names? For whom do they work? If you are interested in finding answers to questions like these, you might turn to J. Valerie Steele's *Washington Representatives* (Washington, D.C.: Columbia Books). This is an annual directory that lists lobbyists, consultants, legal advisers, foreign agents, and public affairs and government relations representatives. The work describes the clients handled by each representative, giving areas of interest and expertise, party affiliation, and ideological orientation. The volume also contains a list of organizations represented in Washington. Finally, it includes a list of selected topics that were cross-referenced so you can find out what companies or associations are likely to be active in what sort of policy discussions.

Public Policy Web Sites. Policy.com at <http://www.policy.com> offers extensive information on pros and cons of current public policy issues. The Electronic Policy Network features a wealth of information on a vast array of public policy issues at its site <http://www.epn.org>. The site is organized by the American

Prospect, a publication with a liberal orientation. On the right, the Cato Institute analyzes public policy issues from a libertarian perspective at <http://www.cato.org/>.

Using Your Knowledge

1. Locate a copy of *Washington Representatives.* What kind of groups take an interest in sugar production? Compare this list with those groups that lobby on women's issues. Which issue (if either) would seem more likely to produce the kind of subsystem described as an iron triangle? Why?

2. Find a public policy issue discussed on Policy.com, the Electonic Policy Network or the Cato Institute Web sites. Summarize the difference in their perspectives on the issue. What kinds of evidence does each use in making its case?

Getting Involved

The Cato Institute offers paid internships. Check their Web site at <http://www.cato.org/jobs/interns.html> to find out more.

Sample Exam Questions

Multiple-Choice Questions

1. A general plan of action used by a government to solve a social problem is called
   a. feedback.
   b. public policy.
   c. oversight.
   d. implementation.

2. Governments that emphasize order tend to specialize in policies that
   a. prohibit.
   b. promote.
   c. protect.
   d. provide.

3. Which of the following is an example of a tax expenditure?
   a. Medicare
   b. Medicaid
   c. The mortgage interest income tax deduction
   d. All of the above

4. Services provided by the government and shared by all residents are called
   a. selective benefits.
   b. tax expenditures.
   c. collective benefits.
   d. off-budget expenditures.

5. Which of the following would be an example of a selective benefit?
   a. The federal highway system
   b. Public education
   c. Food stamps
   d. The Smithsonian Museum

6. Which of the following countries has the highest rate of incarcerating prisoners?
   a. Japan
   b. South Africa
   c. United States
   d. Spain

7. Federalism and the separation of powers contribute to make the policymaking process
    a. fragmented.
    b. majoritarian.
    c. well coordinated.
    d. likely to emphasize order.

8. The study of policy areas concentrates on
    a. policymaking across institutions.
    b. policymaking within institutions.
    c. the majoritarian aspects of American politics.
    d. public sector actors.

9. The term coined to refer to a small, tightly knit subsystem that includes congressional committee leaders, top agency personnel, and lobbyists is
    a. *iron triangle.*
    b. *boondoggle.*
    c. *in-and-outer.*
    d. *issue network.*

10. The increase in interest groups and congressional subcommittees has
    a. increased the power of iron triangles.
    b. closed the policymaking process.
    c. led political scientists to think of these subsystems as issue networks rather than iron triangles.
    d. reduced the requirement that subsystem participants possess technical expertise.

11. Which of the following strategies aims at reducing fragmentation and improving coherence of public policy?
    a. Disbanding interagency task forces
    b. Asking the national government to develop a single regulatory policy
    c. Replacing the OMB with a revamped congressional committee
    d. Developing regulatory policies at the state level

12. In-and-outers
    a. are valued for their experience, know-how, and connections.
    b. have been put out of business by the Ethics in Government Act.
    c. switch jobs often, which keeps their earnings low.
    d. always move from government to the private sector.

13. All issue networks
    a. require participants to have expertise.
    b. operate the same way.
    c. are autonomous, unified, and stable.
    d. are based on consensual, cooperative interaction among participants.

14. Government could cut its size by reducing bureaucrats and not anger people by cutting services because of the
    a. work of nonprofit organizations.
    b. media.
    c. efforts of issue networks.
    d. Internet.

15. It is difficult to significantly reorganize the committee system because of the
    a. opposition of the president.
    b. limited budget.
    c. power of the individual committee chair.
    d. opposition of Republicans.

16. Today, forty percent of the congressional agenda comprises all of the following *except*
    a. environmental regulation.
    b. health care.
    c. foreign trade.
    d. campaign finance.

17. How does the government discover whether or not a policy is working?
    a. Through agenda setting
    b. Through policy formulation
    c. Through implementation
    d. Through policy evaluation

18. The stage of the policymaking process in which new issues are identified as problems to be addressed by government is called
    a. agenda setting.
    b. policy formulation.
    c. implementation.
    d. policy evaluation.

19. Policy formulation may be the result of actions by
    a. Congress.
    b. the president and administrative agencies.
    c. the courts.
    d. all of the above.

20. The implementation stage of the policy process
    a. runs smoothly, because government officials always willingly accept Washington's dictates.
    b. typically involves only Washington bureaucrats.
    c. often involves bargaining and negotiation.
    d. is strictly nonpolitical.

21. Based on the chapter, policy formulation tends to be
    a. radical.
    b. cyclical.
    c. incremental.
    d. none of the above.

22. The part of the policymaking process concerned with carrying out policy is called
    a. agenda setting.
    b. policy formulation.
    c. implementation.
    d. policy evaluation.

23. In contrast with iron triangles, issue networks are likely to involve
    a. less controversial policy questions.
    b. fewer groups or other participants.
    c. narrower policy areas.
    d. more conflict.

24. A key issue in implementation is how much ___ should be given to the state and local officials who have the responsibility of carrying out policies.
    a. regulation
    b. discretion
    c. direction
    d. evaluation

25. The part of the policymaking process in which proposals are developed and officials decide which one, if any, to adopt, is called
    a. agenda setting.
    b. policy formulation.
    c. implementation.
    d. policy evaluation.

Essay Questions

1. Why does the government sometimes pursue conflicting policies? Use specific examples to illustrate your answer.

2. Outline the four basic categories of policy options that governments may adopt to achieve their goals. Give examples of policies in each category.

3. Does government by policy area promote pluralist or majoritarian democracy? Explain your answer and give examples.

4. Why has the concept of the issue network come to replace the iron triangle as a general description of subsystems?

5. How has the emergence of nonprofit organizations facilitated the government?

CHAPTER 18
Economic Policy

Learning Objectives

After reading this chapter you should be able to

- Define the key terms at the end of the chapter.
- Compare and contrast laissez-faire, Keynesian, monetarist, and supply-side economic theory with respect to the role of government in the economy.
- Outline the steps in the budgetary process.
- Show how the Gramm-Rudman Act represented a failure of the legislative and budgetary processes.
- Explain how the Budget Enforcement Act reduced pressure to cut the deficit to meet Gramm-Rudman targets.
- List several possible objectives of tax policy.
- Understand the impact of the stock market.
- Distinguish between progressive and regressive tax policies.
- Compare tax burdens in the United States with those in other Western democracies.
- Assess the effectiveness of American taxing and spending policies in producing greater economic equality.

Economic Policy and the Challenge of Democracy

The opening case illustrates that managing the domestic economy of the United States has become very complicated as a result of globalization, where each country's economy is intertwined with external factors. Making economic public policy, which includes making decisions about taxing and spending, is a value-laden political process. First of all, it involves making choices about the role of government. Should the government maintain more of a hands-off approach, as laissez-faire economists (and, to a lesser extent, supply-siders) believe? Or should it take a more active role?

Public economic policy also requires choices between equality and freedom. The structure of the taxing and spending policies themselves reveals a good bit about the public value system. Whereas Americans are interested in political equality, they are much less committed to economic equality. Americans have moved away from progressive taxation, where the rich pay proportionately more and the tax system serves as a means of redistributing wealth and promoting equality.

One reason why the tax system has not been used to promote greater equality is that the government tends to respond to well-organized and well-financed groups. Thus, pluralist politics have given the wealthy more clout than they might have had under a more majoritarian system.

On the spending side, too, the impact of pluralism is apparent. Incremental budgeting processes have given rise to clientele groups that pressure Congress to keep their favorite programs alive. Other groups managed to get spending programs established firmly by law as entitlement programs. Measures such as the Gramm-Rudman Act and "paygo" restrictions proved inadequate to rein in uncontrollable outlays. The proposed Balanced Budget Amendment narrowly failed. These failures illustrate a problem of the legislative process in a pluralist democracy, where representatives find it too hard to say no to organized groups demanding expenditures or opposing tax increases. The current debate revolves around tax cuts; Democrats and Republicans differ greatly on the size of the tax cut.

Chapter Overview

As a result of the democratization of the stock market, a new president has to be concerned not only about the unemployment rate, but also the stock market. When President Bush came to office in 2001, one of his top priorities was the economy.

Theories of Economic Policy

Taxing and spending are government's two major policy tools for influencing the economy. Their use depends on policymakers' beliefs about how the economy works and how much government should be involved in the economy. Policymakers' (and economists') differences on this issue are rooted in disagreements over economic theories and their assumptions.

Four important schools of thought are used to explain market, or capitalist, economies, where prices are determined through supply and demand.

- *Laissez-faire doctrine* relies on economic competitors to weed out the weak and preserve the strong. Government should not interfere with the economy.
- *Keynesian theory* relies on the government to deal with the problems of depression and inflation by adjusting fiscal policies (government taxing and spending) and monetary policy (the money supply).
- *Monetarism* argues that the adjustments required by Keynesian theory cannot be made quickly enough or at the right time. Political forces make it difficult to cut spending or raise taxes when Keynesian theory requires. Monetarists, therefore, rely on controlling the money supply through the Federal Reserve Board (a more politically independent body) to regulate the business cycle.
- *Supply-side economists* argue that the government should reduce its role in the economy by lowering taxes, thus leaving people with more money. People who have money will invest it in enterprises that will bring them more money. That will create jobs. Tax cuts for the rich will be good for everyone as the benefits "trickle down." Supply-side economics is a partial return to laissez-faire policies. It was also the theoretical underpinning of Reaganomics. In practice, all the predictions of supply-side economics did not come true. In particular, under Reaganomics, while inflation and unemployment came down, tax revenues fell off, and the federal deficit soared. The budget deficits continued until 1998, when an economic boom led to the first budget surplus since 1969.

Public Policy and the Budget

Until 1921, the budget was the principal product of the many congressional committees charged with taxing and spending. The highly decentralized budgeting process was not well adapted to the needs of a growing industrial nation, however. A new process was devised, in which the newly created Bureau of the Budget (later called the Office of Management and Budget, or OMB) helped the president submit budget proposals to Congress. This gave the president the opportunity to set the government's fiscal priorities and take the lead in the budgeting process.

The president's budget is the result of considerable politicking by departments and agencies. The current budgeting process is described as a creaky conglomeration of traditional procedures combined with structural reforms from the 1970s, external constraints from the 1980s, and changes under the 1990 Budget Enforcement Act. The two-step authorization process divides budgeting responsibilities among several committees. This decentralization leaves many opportunities for interest groups to influence the process, and it makes it difficult to assign responsibility for decisions on the budget as a whole.

In the 1970s, Congress attempted to take back some of the control over the budgetary process that it had surrendered to the president. The new process involved structural reforms and a certain amount of coordination among committees, as well as creation of the Congressional Budget Office, a source of expertise equivalent to that of the OMB. The new process broke down, however, when Congress was faced with the huge deficits of the 1980s. Alarmed by the growing deficit, Congress tried something more drastic, the Gramm-Rudman-Hollings Act, which was designed to act as an external constraint and force automatic, across-the-board budget cuts whenever the deficit reached a certain size. The government was unable to meet the Gramm- Rudman deficit-reduction targets, however, and simply revised the target to meet the deficit. Under the pressure of a recession, Congress passed the Budget Enforcement Act of 1990, which caps discretionary spending and places pay-as-you-go restrictions on mandatory spending. This act, together with the 1993 Clinton budget deal paved the way for the Balanced Budget Act of 1997—an agreement that reduced much of the conflict between the parties over fiscal matters.

Tax Policies

Tax policy is designed to provide the money government spends. Government may use tax policy to serve other purposes as well. Tax policy may be used as a method of making tax burdens more equitable or of introducing Keynesian controls on the economy.

In President Reagan's first term, taxes were cut, and the deficit soared. Beginning in his second term, Reagan urged tax reform—lowering taxes in the highest brackets, reducing the number of tax brackets, and eliminating deductions or loopholes, while neither increasing nor decreasing the overall amount of money raised. Tax reform was backed by both Republicans and Democrats. The movement in Congress gathered enough momentum that reform survived, despite pressure from interest groups for special treatment. The result was a somewhat simpler and considerably less progressive two-bracket tax system. Presidents Bush and Clinton each added new brackets at the higher end of the income scale, thereby increasing the progressivity of the tax system. As a result of the budget surpluses, the two major parties debated sharply in the 2000 presidential election on the issue of what to do with the surpluses. The Republicans advocated a large across-the-board tax cut, while the Democrats favored issues like social security reforms, prescription drug coverage for the elderly, and universal health coverage for children.

Although the tax burden on Americans has increased (doubling between 1953 and 1993), this has come about largely because of increases in state and local taxes and social security. Still, in comparison with other democracies, Americans are near the bottom in terms of taxes paid.

Spending Policies

What does the government spend its money on? The largest expenditures go to social security; next comes defense, followed by income security,, and then interest on the national debt. Government spending has increased faster than inflation. However, in recent years, although government spending has increased, the nation's GDP has increased more than spending. Concern with the deficit has checked incremental budgeting, but certain spending programs such as social security and Medicare are difficult to cut because they are legally mandated and backed by politically powerful interests, such as the elderly. Overall, there are very few places left where government spending can be reduced. While the public wants the benefits government provides, it does not want the government to raise taxes to pay for them.

Taxing, Spending, and Economic Equality

Because it requires redistribution of wealth, economic equality can be attained only at the cost of economic freedom. Limited redistribution of wealth through the income tax has aimed at helping the poor reach a minimum standard of living, not at producing overall equality of outcome. In fact, the nation's tax policies as a whole favor the wealthy, especially those who draw their money from investments rather than labor. Although the poor recoup money in transfer payments, regressive taxation claims a higher share of their income. Under capitalism, economic inequality is inevitable, but the degree of inequality may vary. Among Western democracies, the gap between the richest and poorest is largest in America. The United States, which prizes political equality, does not pursue the goal of economic equality with anywhere near the same intensity as other nations. This may be the result of pluralist politics that give upper-income groups more opportunities to exercise influence outside of the "one person, one vote" arena of political equality. Yet, overall, American public opinion shows little support for redistributing wealth through progressive taxation. As a result, even a majoritarian tax policy might do little to reduce inequalities.

Key Terms

economic depression	monetarists	budget committees
inflation	Federal Reserve System	Congressional Budget Office (CB●
business cycle	supply-side economics	Gramm-Rudman
aggregate demand	fiscal year (FY)	mandatory spending
productive capacity	budget authority	entitlement
gross domestic product (GDP)	budget outlays	pay-as-you-go
Keynesian theory	receipts	discretionary spending
fiscal policies	Office of Management and Budget (OMB)	sequestration
monetary policies		progressive taxation
	tax committees	
deficit financing		incremental budgeting
	authorization committees	
Council of Economic Advisers (CEA)		uncontrollable outlay
	appropriations committees	
		transfer payment

Research and Resources

The United States government publishes documents on almost every conceivable topic. People wishing to use these resources were often stymied by the cumbersome cataloging system. With the use of electronic technologies to store more government information, much of this material is now easier to locate and access by using the Internet or CD-ROM technology available at your college or university library.

For an understanding of the national debt, look at www.brillig.com, and click on *U.S. National Debt Clock*.

You can go to www.garnet.berkeley.edu:6997 to get a simulation on the difficulty of balancing the budget.

Using Your Knowledge

1. Using the sites recommended above, track down a government document that provides you with information on one of the following subjects:

   - the anti-flag-burning amendment
   - NATO expansion
   - tax reform

2. A major concern of the text is political values. As this chapter indicates, two important sources of information about the values of a society are its tax code and its government's budget. The taxing and spending policies of a nation give people incentives to do some things but not others. To gain insight into American values, do one of the following:

   - Obtain a copy of the filing instructions for the federal income tax. You can find IRS forms on-line at <http://www.irs.ustreas.gov/basic/forms_pubs/index.html>. Look at the deductions allowed.

What activities does the tax code seem to encourage? Do these tax regulations seem more likely to be the result of majoritarian or pluralist politics?

- Obtain a copy of the *Budget of the United States Government.* Visit <http://www.access.gpo. gov/su_docs/budget/index.html>. Page (or scroll) through and examine the spending categories and the kinds of activities the government funds. Do these expenditures seem more likely to be the result of majoritarian or pluralist politics? Why?

Sample Exam Questions

Multiple-Choice Questions

1. The economic theory that relies on the narrow pursuit of individual profit to serve the broader ends of society through an invisible-hand mechanism was associated first with
    a. Adam Smith.
    b. Arthur Laffer.
    c. John Maynard Keynes.
    d. Milton Friedman.

2. Many business executives credit this official rather than the president with the economic prosperity of the 1990s.
    a. The chairman of the Federal Reserve Board
    b. The vice president
    c. The chairman of the Council of Economic Advisors
    d. The speaker of the House

3. Economies that rely on government planners to determine the prices of goods and the quantities to be produced are called
    a. nonmarket economies.
    b. capitalist economies.
    c. laissez-faire economies.
    d. market economies.

4. Cutting or increasing government spending to control business cycles is an example of the use of
    a. monetarism.
    b. fiscal policies.
    c. laissez faire.
    d. deficit financing.

5. Which of the following is correct concerning the CPI?
    a. It is an accurate and impartial measure of inflation.
    b. It usually underestimates inflation.
    c. If it overestimates inflation, retirees on social security will receive larger allotments.
    d. If it underestimates inflation, union workers will receive larger pay raises.

6. To deal with problems of inflation and unemployment, monetarists would rely heavily on
    a. the fiscal tools of Keynesian economics.
    b. laissez-faire principles.
    c. use of the Federal Reserve System.
    d. supply-side economics.

7. The economic theory that suggests that lowering taxes and reducing government intervention will increase productivity and yield more tax revenue is associated with
   a. *perestroika.*
   b. Keynesian economics.
   c. monetarism.
   d. supply-side economics.

8. The traditional two-step budget process of authorization and appropriation offered rich opportunities for the practice of
   a. majoritarian democracy.
   b. pluralist democracy.
   c. presidential power.
   d. judicial review.

9. Which of the following congressional committees are involved in budgeting?
   a. Tax committees
   b. Authorization committees
   c. Appropriations committees
   d. All of the above

10. A tax system that requires wealthier people to pay a higher percentage of their income in taxes is known as
    a. regressive.
    b. progressive.
    c. revenue-neutral.
    d. flat.

11. Since the end of the Cold War, economic orthodoxy held that countries should do all of the following *except*
    a. liberalize trade.
    b. restrain public spending.
    c. privatize state property.
    d. spend more on the military.

12. Which of the following is the smallest component of the federal budget?
    a. Defense spending
    b. Foreign aid
    c. Interest on the national debt
    d. Income security programs

13. In general, taking national, state, and local systems together, the U.S. tax system
    a. takes a higher proportion of the GNP than do the systems of other democracies.
    b. is progressive.
    c. is regressive.
    d. has relied on income tax for practically all of its revenue.

14. Which of the following has historically been an example of progressive taxation?
    a. The social security tax
    b. State sales taxes
    c. The federal income tax
    d. All of the above

15. On the whole, American tax policies favor which group the *most*?
    a. The wealthy who draw their income from capital
    b. Middle-class workers
    c. The poor on welfare
    d. The working poor

16. When agencies draft a budget asking for the amount they received in the current year plus an additional amount for new programs, they are engaged in
    a. incremental budgeting.
    b. discretionary spending.
    c. mandatory spending.
    d. zero-based budgeting.

17. Economies in which the prices of goods and services are determined through the interaction of sellers and buyers are called
    a. nonmarket economies.
    b. market economies.
    c. mixed economies.
    d. directed economies.

18. Which of the following would be an unlikely policy for a Keynesian to adopt to control the business cycle?
    a. Raise taxes
    b. Lower taxes
    c. Increase the money supply
    d. Use a laissez-faire approach

19. The Federal Reserve Board may use any of the following mechanisms to control the money supply *except*
    a. changing the reserve requirements.
    b. changing the discount rate.
    c. changing the income tax rate.
    d. buying and selling government securities.

20. The amount of money a government agency is authorized to spend for programs is called its
    a. off-budget expenditure.
    b. tax expenditure.
    c. budget authority.
    d. budget outlay.

21. A national sales tax or value-added tax would be an example of a(n)
    a. progressive tax.
    b. revenue-neutral tax.
    c. regressive tax.
    d. unconstitutional use of the national government's taxing power.

22. Democratization of stocks means that a president now should be concerned about all of the following *except* the
    a. unemployment rate.
    b. Dow Jones Industrial Average.
    c. NASDAQ.
    d. Russian military build-up.

23. The economic theory that relies on fiscal policies to adjust demand and thereby reduce fluctuations in the business cycle is
    a. laissez-faire economics.
    b. supply-side economics.
    c. socialist economics.
    d. Keynesian economics.

24. In the election of 2000, the two major parties differed sharply on all of the following issues *except*
    a. tax cuts.
    b. social security reforms.
    c. the best use of the surplus.
    d. U.S. policy in Kosovo.

25. Government payments to individuals, such as social security payments, unemployment compensation, and food stamps are known as
    a. discretionary spending.
    b. controllable spending.
    c. transfer payments.
    d. tax expenditures.

Essay Questions

1. Explain the difference between progressive and regressive taxes. Is a flat tax progressive or regressive? Why?

2. What is supply-side economics? How does it differ from standard Keynesian economics?

3. What were the goals of Reaganomics? How well were they achieved?

4. Why is the United States more economically unequal than other Western democracies?

5. Which should be given more priority—a tax cut or paying off the national debt?

CHAPTER 19
Domestic Policy

Learning Objectives

After reading this chapter you should be able to

- Define the key terms at the end of the chapter.
- Trace the growth of the American welfare state.
- Discuss the debates on social security.
- Indicate who pays for and who benefits from the social security system.
- Explain how social welfare policies involve tradeoffs between equality and freedom.
- Discuss the reasons why the United States, unlike other industrialized nations, has not adopted a system of universal health coverage.
- Distinguish between social insurance programs and public assistance programs.
- Describe changes made in the welfare system by the 1996 welfare reform law.
- Compare the costs and benefits of the American system of social welfare with the systems in other democratic states.

Domestic Policy and the Challenge of Democracy

This chapter highlights the inevitable difficulty of balancing competing values when the government adopts public policy. Social insurance and welfare policies, for example, raise a conflict between equality and freedom.

Before the Great Depression, most aid for the poor came from private charities rather than the government. Old people got by on their savings or on private pensions rather than government-sponsored social security. By 1934, many states provided old-age assistance programs, but the economic hardships of the 1930s far outstripped the ability of such programs and of private charities to cope. National relief efforts had to be launched. As a result, people's attitudes about the role of government started to change. Throughout most of American history, the government had confined its activities to protecting persons and property, thereby providing security and order. In the thirties, people began to accept the idea that government should provide a kind of economic floor to protect people from falling into abject poverty.

The New Deal of the 1930s and the Great Society of the 1960s created many programs for aiding the poor. These programs' costs were shouldered by taxpayers, which set up a conflict between freedom and equality. On the one hand, citizens may accept the notion that the government should help the poor; on the other hand, they may resent the loss of freedom to control the part of their income that goes to pay higher taxes. With the end of the Cold War, social welfare and economy have moved to the forefront of voters' concerns.

Before the Depression, people who relied on others for charity were often seen as moral failures. But the poverty of the Depression was so widespread that it challenged this idea. Eventually, many federal aid programs were viewed as "entitlements," and aid recipients worked to protect the programs important to them. The domestic aid programs discussed in this chapter show pluralist politics in action. Older Americans of retirement age exercise enormous political power and are keenly interested in protecting the social security and Medicare programs. Under the recent welfare reform law, however, those defending the poor have suffered setbacks in preserving welfare as an entitlement.

Chapter Overview

The chapter illustrates how policies that provide social insurance or public assistance raise conflicts between the values of freedom, order, and equality.

These areas of public policy aim at alleviating some of the consequences of economic inequality. Government expenditures in these areas represent more than half the national budget of the United States. These huge expenditures to promote equality also stimulate conflicts of values, since government policies that redistribute resources lessen individual freedom.

Government Policies and Individual Welfare

Virtually every modern nation is a welfare state—providing for its citizens through economic and social programs. Although social welfare programs date back to the Industrial Revolution, the modern welfare state received its impetus from the Great Depression and the New Deal, the Roosevelt administration's attempt to manage the crisis. The New Deal had two phases. The first aimed at relief from the Depression itself by boosting prices and lowering unemployment. The second phase was more concerned with long-term reform and included a program of social insurance to aid the poor and the aged. The New Deal abandoned reliance on laissez-faire capitalism and a decentralized federal structure. Instead it emphasized more central-government control of the economy, and it set in motion long-term trends toward government expansion.

In the 1960s, President Lyndon Johnson launched the Great Society to combat political, social, and economic inequality through civil rights legislation, aid to education, and the War on Poverty. Though most of its programs disappeared during the Vietnam War, the War on Poverty did make the poor aware of their political power.

Social welfare is based on the premise that society has an obligation to provide for the basic needs of its members. In the 1980s, President Reagan questioned this assumption and shifted the emphasis from economic equality to economic freedom. This meant a reexamination of many federal social welfare programs. Tight federal budgets have continued to make funds scarce for initiating or enlarging social welfare programs.

Social Insurance

In America, social insurance programs are entitlements—benefits to which every eligible person has a legal right that the government cannot deny. The largest federal entitlement program is social security, an insurance program that provides economic assistance to the unemployed, disabled, and aged without regard to their financial need.

Many European states adopted programs like social security after World War I; in the United States, the Social Security Act of 1935 was passed as part of the second phase of the New Deal. Money for the old-age benefits of social security are paid into a trust fund. Under a pay-as-you-go tax system, today's workers support today's elderly. When the program started, only a few people received benefits while many contributed. Over the years, however, the ratio of workers to benefit recipients has decreased. Meanwhile, social security benefits have increased, partly through cost-of-living adjustments (COLAs) enthusiastically supported by both political parties in the 1970s. Government officials expected to be able to finance these increases out of economic growth, but "stagflation" made that impossible. As a result, it became necessary to increase social security taxes and reduce benefits. Although the future effects of economic conditions on the social security system are hard to predict, few people argue about the need for the system. In the presidential election campaign, the Republicans proposed that individuals should be allowed to invest their own payroll taxes in the stock market with the possibility of higher return. The Democrats proposed a private investment program in which government would match individual contributions with tax credits.

In the 1960s, as a part of Lyndon Johnson's Great Society, Congress approved Medicare, a program of medical insurance for the elderly, and Medicaid, a need-based health program for the poor. These programs, too, have faced financial problems, as medical costs have soared. New procedures were introduced in 1985 to provide hospitals with incentives to keep costs down.

While Medicare and Medicaid provide health care for the aged and the poor, increased health-care costs and difficulties of obtaining insurance helped put the issue of health care for all on the agenda. Yet, as the Clinton administration and Congress approached the issue, it proved difficult to forge a consensus on the form health-care policy should take. Health care raises the modem dilemma of government, which pits equality against freedom.

Public Assistance

Public assistance, often called welfare, is government aid to individuals based on their need. In addition to establishing the old-age insurance program described above, the Social Security Act created categorical assistance programs for needy people who are old, blind, disabled, or have dependent children. These entitlement programs are funded jointly by federal and state tax revenues. Though the bulk of the funding comes from the national government, benefits vary from state to state. Until 1996, national standards were imposed on state programs. These standards established the national poverty level, which still helps measure how well public policies manage to achieve the American promise of equality. The poverty line also leads to the ambiguity on the concept of equality.

Two key programs—food stamps and cash payments—attempt to address the problem of poverty. The food stamp program, which supplements recipients' food-purchasing power, aims at meeting the nutritional needs of the poor. The range of people entitled to food stamps has shrunk recently, as illegal aliens and unemployed people not raising children have been excluded. Food stamp benefits are set by the national government. In 1996, President Clinton and the Republican-led Congress produced compromise legislation that radically changed welfare. The new law ended Aid to Families with Dependent Children (AFDC), barred noncitizens from receiving welfare payments, and introduced work requirements and limits on the length of time people can receive benefits. States received greater latitude to shape their own welfare systems with block grants of funds provided by Washington. The changes are controversial, but, aided by a booming economy, they produced a rapid drop in the welfare rolls. Whether the reforms reduce inequality in the long run remains to be seen.

Education and Equality

Based on the presidential election of 2000, education has come to the center stage. The debate on education concerns the dilemma of freedom versus equality. Traditional policy on education centered on providing equal access, however, Republicans have recently proposed increased freedom and choice for families.

Benefits and Fairness

The government offers both means-tested and non-means-tested benefits to Americans. As program costs increase, many people believe that it might be fairer to apportion benefits according to need.

Key Terms

public policy	prescription drug care coverage	Social Security Act
welfare state	War on Poverty	health maintenance organization (HMO)
social welfare programs	"feminization of poverty"	
Great Depression	social insurance	preferred provider organization (PPO)
New Deal	entitlements	Medicare
Great Society	social security	public assistance

poverty level

food stamp program

non-means-tested benefits

Temporary Assistance for
  Needy Families Act (TANF)

means-tested benefits

Head Start

Research and Resources

Virtually every American is affected by the public policies described in this chapter. The programs themselves were created by acts of Congress, but as you learned in Chapter 12, Congress does not specify every detail concerning every program. Instead, Congress leaves a considerable amount of discretion to the agencies charged with administering programs. These agencies make rules and establish procedures. But how can a citizen find out what the rules are? They are published in a government publication called the *Federal Register*. Since 1995, the *Federal Register* has been available on-line in a searchable form, which overcomes many of the difficulties of the older, printed version. The URL for the homepage of the *Federal Register* is <http://www.access.gpo.gov/su_docs/aces/aces140.html>.

The printed version of the *Federal Register* can be difficult to use, but the government has issued a user's guide to it. Instructions may also be found in *Congressional Quarterly's Federal Regulatory Directory*. The *Federal Register* is published daily. It includes "notices of proposed rule making," that is, agency proposals for new rules; these must be publicized before they can be implemented. When a proposed rule is adopted by an agency, it must be published again as a "final rule." Federal rules undergo constant revision. Each year, the rules of all the agencies are collected into a set of volumes called the *Code of Federal Regulations* (CFR) that can be found on-line at <http://www.access.gpo.gov/nara/cfr/index.html>. The CFR assigns "title numbers" to broad subject areas affected by regulatory action; for example, Title 7 deals with agriculture, and Title 45 deals with public welfare. Each title is broken down into chapters (designated by Roman numerals), and the chapters are further subdivided into numbered parts. For example, the rules and regulations of the Drug Enforcement Administration would be found in Title 21, Chapter XIII, Part 1300 to the end of the title.

One relatively easy way to locate an agency's regulations is to use the *Federal Regulatory Directory*, which includes as part of its description the CFR titles and parts used by agencies.

The following example should give you an idea of a method for looking up regulations in paper volumes. Work through each step outlined here. Suppose you wanted to find out if full-time college students are eligible to receive food stamps. First, you would need to know what agency administers the food stamp program. If you look under the words *food stamps* in the index of the *Federal Regulatory Directory*, you will learn that the program is administered by an agency called the Food and Nutrition Service, which is part of the Department of Agriculture. If you read through the description of that agency, you will see a section marked "Rules and Regulations." That section tells you where to look in the *Code of Federal Regulations* to find the rules affecting this agency and its programs. Specifically, it directs you to Title 7, Parts 210–299 of the CFR. If you obtain the volume of the CFR containing Title 7, Parts 210–299, you will find a table of contents directing you to subchapter C, "Food Stamp and Food Distribution Program." The part most useful to you appears to be Part 273, "Certification of eligible households," which includes a section (§273.5) labeled "Students" that outlines the eligibility requirements students must satisfy to receive food stamps. With on-line searching, entering the words "students" *and* "food stamps" will lead you to the same result and allow you to retrieve the text of the regulation instantly.

Using Your Knowledge

Use the *Code of Federal Regulations* to find the following:

- student eligibility requirements for Pell grants
- the parity price of tobacco
- regulations governing access to the Internet for schools and libraries

Getting Involved

Founded in 1981, the Center on Budget and Policy Priorities works on public policy issues affecting low-income families and individuals. They have full- and part-time paid internships available for undergraduate and graduate students. Learn more about these opportunities at their Web site, <http://www.cbpp.org/internship.html>. The Children's Defense Fund offers internships on policy matters dealing with children, such as improving child health, nutrition, and the availability of child care. Find out more at their Web site at <http://www.childrensdefense.org/intern_positions.html>.

Sample Exam Questions

Multiple-Choice Questions

1. Pell grants are an example of a
   a. collective benefit.
   b. means-tested benefit.
   c. non-means-tested benefit.
   d. social insurance program.

2. The Great Society included programs aimed at
   a. eliminating political inequality.
   b. eliminating social inequality.
   c. eliminating economic inequality.
   d. doing all of the above.

3. A reexamination of social welfare policy, with a shift in emphasis from economic equality to economic freedom, began under President
   a. Franklin Roosevelt.
   b. John Kennedy.
   c. Lyndon Johnson.
   d. Ronald Reagan.

4. Social security is an example of
   a. an entitlement program.
   b. a "pay-as-you-go" program.
   c. a compulsory insurance program.
   d. all of the above.

5. From 1972 through the end of that decade, social security benefits rose
   a. despite a lack of political clout on the part of the elderly.
   b. because Congress voted annual adjustments in excess of the cost of living.
   c. due to automatic cost-of-living adjustments.
   d. because social security is an entitlement program.

6. The social insurance program that provides medical care for the aged is
   a. called Medicaid.
   b. completely voluntary.
   c. completely compulsory.
   d. called Medicare.

7. The minimum cash income that will provide for a family's basic needs is referred to as the
   a. entitlement level.
   b. poverty level.
   c. categorical assistance level.
   d. public assistance level.

8. Until it was abolished in 1996, the largest public assistance program was
   a. aid to the needy elderly.
   b. aid to the needy blind.
   c. aid to the disabled.
   d. Aid to Families with Dependent Children.

9. In the 2000 election, Republicans argued that if the system were not changed, the country would be forced to do all of the following *except*
   a. raise taxes.
   b. reduce benefits.
   c. add to the national debt.
   d. cut social security taxes.

10. Under the welfare reform measures passed in 1996,
    a. most noncitizens will become ineligible for benefits.
    b. uniform work requirements must be established in all states.
    c. uniform benefit payment levels must be established in all states.
    d. all of the above are true.

11. Which of the following contributed to the "feminization of poverty"?
    a. The increased divorce rate
    b. The lack of affordable child care
    c. Increases in teenage pregnancy
    d. All of the above

12. Supporters of a national system of health care are *most* likely to prefer which of the following?
    a. Freedom over order
    b. Order over freedom
    c. Equality over freedom
    d. Equality over order

13. Public opinion polls during the presidential election of 2000 showed that fully one-half of the American electorate believed this to be an extremely important issue.
    a. Education
    b. Health care
    c. Crime
    d. Foreign policy

14. Individual benefit programs such as AFDC, food stamps, and social security were
    a. designed to produce equality of outcome.
    b. designed to provide the minimum living conditions necessary.
    c. available only to the deserving poor.
    d. all based on need.

15. As a result of welfare reform,
    a. the economy is booming.
    b. states have had to increase their numbers of case workers to keep up with increased case loads.
    c. the number of people on welfare has declined.
    d. welfare recipients may not receive job placement assistance.

16. Most poor families are headed by
    a. African Americans.
    b. women.
    c. whites.
    d. Hispanics.

17. Social welfare policy in America is based on the premise that
    a. society has an obligation to provide for the minimum welfare of its members.
    b. the government should take from each according to his or her ability and give to each according to his or her need.
    c. laissez- faire systems are best.
    d. no redistribution of wealth should take place in a just society.

18. Under social security, retirement benefits
    a. are distributed on the basis of need only.
    b. are distributed without regard for need.
    c. automatically include food stamps.
    d. are paid for from income tax revenue.

19. Social security is called a pay-as-you-go system. This means that
    a. today's workers support today's elderly.
    b. you pay in while you are working, and the money is saved until you retire.
    c. it is a progressive tax.
    d. it is financed out of income taxes.

20. Since the social security program began, the tax rate has
    a. increased and the number of workers covered has decreased.
    b. increased and the ratio of workers to recipients has shrunk.
    c. decreased as more workers have been included.
    d. decreased because the benefits have decreased.

21. Data on health expenditures and longevity show that
    a. the larger a country's per capita health expenditures, the longer its citizens will live.
    b. the larger a country's total health expenditures, the longer its citizens will live.
    c. the smaller a country's per capita health expenditures, the longer its citizens will live.
    d. health expenditures do not seem to be closely related to longevity.

22. The social insurance program that aids the disabled, old, and unemployed and is financed by taxes on employees and employers is
    a. Medicaid.
    b. AFDC.
    c. social security.
    d. food stamps.

23. The major impetus for the creation of America's social security system came from
    a. the Civil War.
    b. World War I.
    c. the Great Depression.
    d. the War on Poverty.

24. In the 2000 election, the Republican platform included all of the following *except*
    a. raising academic standards through increased local control.
    b. greater flexibility in school choice.
    c. parental control.
    d. federal control.

25. In the 2000 election, the Democratic platform proposed all of the following *except*
    a. requiring all teachers to pass a competency exam.
    b. providing school vouchers.
    c. improving technology in classrooms.
    d. making pre-school affordable to all families.

Essay Questions

1. How did the Great Depression help produce new attitudes about the government's role in ensuring the social welfare of citizens?

2. What methods did the War on Poverty use in its effort to eradicate poverty?

3. Compare and contrast the Democratic and Republican platforms on education reforms. What were the merits and demerits of each platform?

4. Are public assistance programs equally available to everyone in America? Explain your answer.

5. The United States is the only major industrialized nation without a universal health-care system. What key problems have those who have sought to create such a system in America encountered?

CHAPTER 20
Global Policy

<hr>

Learning Objectives

After reading this chapter you should be able to

- Define the key terms at the end of the chapter.
- Describe the changes in outlook and priorities that characterized America's emergence as a super-power following World War II.
- Outline the basic consensus that characterized American foreign policy during the Cold War.
- Explain why that consensus broke down.
- Show how foreign policy issues have become more "intermestic" since the end of the Cold War.
- Differentiate between "high politics" and "low politics."
- Discuss the impact of trade and investment policies on foreign policy.
- Outline the president's chief powers in the area of foreign policy, and list the devices presidents have used to avoid congressional limitations on those powers.
- Describe the roles played by the Department of State, Department of Defense, National Security Council, and Central Intelligence Agency in making foreign policy.
- Identify other players in the foreign policymaking process.
- Assess the limits of public opinion as a guide for foreign policy.

Global Policy and the Challenge of Democracy

The opening vignette suggests that not only members of Congress but also private individuals and organizations affect U.S. foreign policy. The end of the Cold War has offered the opportunity to create a "New World Order." How will the United States respond to this challenge? The answer is not yet clear. The text has maintained throughout that majoritarian politics and clear agreements on values do not really characterize American politics generally, so it should be no surprise to find them missing in the area of foreign policy. And yet, at least from World War II to the Vietnam War, presidents did enjoy bipartisan support based on fundamental agreement within the country about the appropriate goals for American foreign policy and the appropriate means of conducting it. Politics "stopped at the water's edge." Today, policymakers usually agree that our primary goal is to protect American national security, but they disagree over the nature of the threats to that security and the best means to defend it. Policymakers may want a stable world order. They may also want economic prosperity. But achieving these goals may lead America to oppose revolutionary movements in the developing world or to support regimes that violate human rights. Should we choose stability (order) over freedom? In the short run, at least, it is possible to maintain order through the use of force; but in the long run, many argue, stability is best preserved by rooting out the sort of political and social inequalities that lead to disorder.

Other questions about values raised in connection with foreign policy concern the cost of superpower status. What does it cost to be a superpower—not just in dollars, but in terms of other values important to democracy? How much freedom do we give up at home by tolerating the secrecy of the Central Intelligence Agency (CIA)? How should decisions about foreign policy be made in a democracy? Analysts like de Tocqueville certainly feared the application of a majoritarian model, which would make impossible the consistency and secrecy required in foreign affairs. While recent research has suggested that the American public is generally consistent in its foreign policy views and responsive to candidates' foreign policy positions, it is still hard to see the making of foreign policy as the outcome of a majoritarian process.

Certainly the foreign policy area is full of examples of pluralistic politics in action. Ethnic groups, foreign governments, businesses, and unions may all lobby in support of foreign policy interests. But in foreign policy, the president still remains the most important actor.

Chapter Overview

Following World War II, the United States built a consensus foreign policy on the need to overcome Soviet-inspired communist aggression everywhere in the world. With the fall of the Soviet Union and the end of the Cold War, this objective is no longer relevant. America needs to shape a new approach to foreign policy. That approach may emphasize new issues—such as trade and the environment—the issues of "low politics," centered on such concerns as trade and the environment, in addition to those of "high politics," which revolve around defense and military security.

Making Foreign Policy: The Constitutional Context

Under the Constitution, the president is clearly the chief actor in foreign policy matters; but, as elsewhere in the system, Congress has several prerogatives that serve as checks on his powers. However, presidents have frequently used tools like executive agreements, undeclared wars, transfer authority, reprogramming, and special envoys to sidestep constitutional limitations on their foreign policy powers.

A Review of Foreign Policy

The Monroe Doctrine of 1823, which advocated an isolationist policy and nonintervention in European politics, dominated the U.S. foreign policy in most of the nineteenth century. World War II and its aftermath brought a decisive change, as globalism replaced isolationism. Following the war, the United States adopted a policy of containment to limit Soviet expansion. The pillars of containment were the Bretton-Woods economic system, the Marshall Plan, and the NATO alliance. Containment required creation of a much larger military and a commitment to far higher levels of defense spending.

In the first decade or so of containment policy, the United States relied heavily on nuclear deterrence to hold the Soviets in check. The shift from near-exclusive reliance on nuclear deterrence to flexible response under President Kennedy created a need for greater military spending. In addition, Kennedy committed himself to nation-building policies in the developing world.

The commitment the United States made to nation building in Vietnam cost well over 58,000 American lives and badly damaged America's foreign policy consensus.

While the Vietnam War continued, President Nixon pursued a policy of détente toward the Soviet Union and also opened the way for relations with the People's Republic of China. The post-Vietnam era saw Jimmy Carter's attempt to base foreign policy on human rights and Ronald Reagan's reemphasis on military strength and anticommunism as the backbone of U.S. foreign policy. With the decline of communism in Eastern Europe, America's chief adversary has paled in strength. But no clear, consistent foreign-policy vision has emerged to help policymakers balance the conflicting demands of establishing a stable world order, promoting the creation of free institutions, and creating a level of international economic equality adequate to protect against instability.

From Foreign to Global Policy

Foreign policy focuses on security against military threats. On the other hand, global policy focuses on social and environmental concerns. In global policy, the players are no longer competing alliances but international organizations that cooperate internationally.

Global Issue Areas

In the post-Cold War era, defense and military issues continue to be important. The collapse of communism has allowed the United States to make defense cutbacks, but new security threats have emerged as America attempts to define its role as the world's only superpower. The country is fashioning new institutional structures, such as an enlarged NATO. The end of the Cold War has shifted attention to new foreign policy issue areas that highlight the extent to which America exists in an interdependent community of nations. Economically, the United States is linked to the rest of the world through aid, trade, and investment. Environmentally, Americans are finding that the choices and activities of one nation may have an ecological impact on the rest of the world. Finally, the beginning of a New World Order challenges the United States to examine its commitment to human rights and the relationship of this value to other policy priorities.

Making Foreign Policy: Organization and Cast

The major organizations responsible for formulating and conducting foreign affairs are the Department of State, the Department of Defense, the National Security Council, and the CIA. The Department of State has the most to do with the overall conduct of foreign affairs, yet it has a relatively small staff (certainly in comparison with the Department of Defense) and has often been criticized for its inertia. The Department of Defense manages America's military forces and provides civilian control over the military. The CIA is charged with gathering intelligence about the actions or intentions of foreign powers. It also performs certain covert operations. These activities have given rise to controversies about the place of such operations in a democratic government. In response, Congress placed legislative limits and reporting requirements on CIA operations. The National Security Council (NSC) coordinates the details of foreign, military, and domestic policy as they relate to national security. Due to globalization and interdependence of social, environmental, and economic issues with political matters, the number of players involved in making foreign policy has increased, to include the Departments of Commerce and Agriculture as well as offices set up by state governments.

The Public and Foreign Policy

Historically, the public has paid little attention to traditional concerns of foreign policy issues. Recently, however, there has been a steady increase in the percentage of people who believe the United States should play an active part in world affairs. The making of foreign policy does not closely adhere to majority rule. Interest groups—including ethnic groups, business groups, unions, and others—are becoming increasingly involved in the process. The media also help shape the process, particularly through their function as agenda setters.

Key Terms

high politics	North Atlantic Treaty Organization (NATO)	nontariff barriers (NTBs)
Cold War		managed trade
	Third World	
low politics		protectionist
	nation building	
intermestic		big emerging markets (BEMs)
	détente	
sovereign		executive agreement
	comparative advantage	
containment		War Powers Resolution

Research and Resources

What is U.S. policy toward Myanmar, or Morocco, or Burkina Faso, or Argentina? You can find the answers by consulting *Background Notes on Countries of the World,* a series of loose-leaf publications prepared by the Department of State. This material is also accessible on-line through the State Department's Web page at <http://www.state.gov/www/background_notes/>. These notes give information on the history, population, economy, and government of every nation in the world, with a summary of the current status of each nation's relations with the United States. They are also very useful for travelers. The Department of State's Web site also provides information on policy issues as well as policy toward nations and regions. Check their home page at <http://www.state.gov/>.

What about defense policy? Where can you find information on defense and foreign policy? Start with the Department of Defense's official Web site at <http://www.defenselink.mil/>. How do you discover how American defense spending compares with the defense spending of other nations? Try *World Military Expenditures and Arms Transfers,* published annually by the U.S. Arms Control and Disarmament Agency, a part of the federal government. Another interesting source for research into weapons systems is the *Defense and Foreign Affairs Handbook* (Washington, D.C.: Defense and Foreign Affairs, Ltd.), which includes descriptions of the defense capabilities of nations around the globe. It offers a handy guide to "who's who in politics and defense," as well as a list of corporations that supply armaments to the government and descriptions of the kinds of products they supply. SIPRI, the Stockholm International Peace Research Institute, publishes an annual yearbook on armaments, disarmaments, and international security. Much of their data is available on-line through their Web site at <http://sunsite.sipri.se/>. For a respected source critical of defense spending, try Center for Defense Information at <http:www.cdi.org>. For a pro-defense spin, you might also visit the Heritage Foundation's National Security site at <http://www.nationalsecurity.org/>.

Using Your Knowledge

1. Select an important foreign policy issue (such as U.S. policy toward Kosovo or the Global Warming Convention). Visit the Department of State's Web site to find current U.S. policy. Have there been debates in Congress on the issue? Finally, research public opinion on the issue.

2. Using Internet resources, trace U.S. defense spending over the past decade. How does it compare to the defense spending of other NATO nations?

Getting Involved

Careers in Foreign Affairs

Students interested in careers in international affairs often hope to work for the Department of State. As this chapter points out, the bad news is that positions as foreign-service officers are highly competitive. There is good news, though—namely, that there are many other opportunities to work for the U.S. government in the area of international affairs. There are also opportunities to be involved in international affairs working for nongovernmental organizations.

Foreign Service. As the text mentions, the first hurdle for those seeking a foreign-service appointment in the Department of State is a written examination. To obtain further information, visit the Department of State's Careers Web site at <http://www.state.gov/www/careers/index.html>.

Other Departments in International Affairs. There are many other ways to pursue a career in international affairs. Here is a short list of other federal departments and agencies that deal with international matters.

The Department of Agriculture runs international affairs and commodity programs as well as marketing and inspection programs. Try contacting the department's employment office at Room 1080, South Building, Washington, D.C. 20250 or the Personnel Division, Field Servicing Office, Animal and Plant Inspection Service, USDA, 100 N. Sixth St., Butler Square West, Minneapolis, MN 55403.

To learn more about positions with the CIA, write to Recruitment Center, ATTN: DST/AAT Rep, P.O. Box 12727, Dept., Arlington VA 22209-8727 or visit their Web site, "Innovation and Intrigue: Employment at the CIA" at <http://www.odci.gov/cia/employment/ciaindex.htm>.

You might be interested in the International Trade Administration of the Department of Commerce. This organization tries to promote overseas markets for U.S. goods. The address is Personnel Office, Room 4808, Hoover Building, 14th St. and Constitution Ave., NW, Washington, D.C. 20230.

The Peace Corps at <http://www.peacecorps.gov/> accepts volunteers for two-year terms in over 70 countries. The agency also has its own staff of regular employees overseeing operations. For further information, contact the Peace Corps, Office of Personnel, 1990 K St., NW, Washington, D.C. 20526.

Internships

As you contemplate a career in the field of international affairs or foreign policy, you may want to take a closer look. Some of the possibilities for internships in government, as well as in think tanks and with interest groups include the following.

With the U.S. Government. The Department of State offers both paid summer internships and work-study internships. These internships are highly competitive and may even include work overseas. The lead time for obtaining Department of State internships is fairly long, since successful applicants may need to be put through a security clearance. Applications for summer are usually due around November 1. For further information, visit their Web page at <http://www.state.gov/www/careers/rinterncontents.html>.

The CIA offers internships paid at the rate of $300 to $375 per week. These are available at its Langley, Virginia, headquarters as well as elsewhere. Its undergraduate internships are open to minority and disabled students in their junior and senior years of college. Applications for summer spots are due early—September 30! For more information, write to the Central Intelligence Agency, CIA Employment Center, P.O. Box 12727, Arlington, VA 22209.

The Peace Corps also offers a year-round, two- to six-month internship program in its headquarters offices. These internships are unpaid. Applicants must submit a Standard Form 171 Personal Qualifications Statement. For further information, contact the Student Intern Coordinator, Peace Corps Personnel, 806 Connecticut Avenue, NW, Room P-307, Washington, D.C. 20526. Telephone: (800) 424-8580.

Internships outside Government. The Center for Defense Information gives students with an interest in defense policy and related public-policy issues the opportunity to serve as research and outreach assistants. These competitive, paid internships are offered in spring, summer, and fall. The deadlines are October 15 for spring, March 15 for summer, and July 1 for fall. For further information, visit their Web site at <http://www.cdi.org> or contact the Intern Coordinator, Center for Defense Information, 1779 Massachusetts Avenue, NW, Washington, D.C. 20036.

The Kathryn and Shelby Cullom Davis International Studies Center, a department of the Heritage Foundation, conducts research and publishes papers on a wide variety of international political, economic, and security issues and offers internships during the fall and spring semesters. To find out more, send e-mail to <froningd@heritage.org>.

Sample Exam Questions

Multiple-Choice Questions

1. The breakdown in America's foreign policy consensus came as a result of
   a. World War II.
   b. the Korean conflict.
   c. the Cuban Missile Crisis.
   d. the Vietnam War.

2. Which of the following would *not* usually be considered "low politics"?
   a. A trade agreement
   b. Discussion of a biodiversity treaty
   c. Bilateral discussions of reductions in U.S. troops stationed abroad
   d. A UN conference on population

3. The nineteenth-century doctrine that outlined an essentially isolationist course for the United States vis-à-vis Europe was the
   a. Madison Doctrine.
   b. Monroe Doctrine.
   c. Rush-Bagot Treaty.
   d. Wilson Doctrine.

4. Nation-states are called sovereign when they
   a. owe obedience to no power or law other than their own.
   b. have a queen.
   c. have a positive balance of trade.
   d. are economically self-sufficient and do not need to trade.

5. The Kennedy administration's policy of developing many different capabilities to create a range of options in a crisis situation was known as
   a. nation building.
   b. flexible response.
   c. mutual assured destruction.
   d. détente.

6. The North Atlantic Treaty committed the United States to
   a. the defense of Vietnam.
   b. the defense of Western Europe.
   c. end the draft.
   d. cut defense spending.

7. The policy that committed the United States to stopping Soviet expansion was called
   a. the Marshall Plan.
   b. flexible response.
   c. containment.
   d. mutual assured destruction.

8. The relationship between the United States and the Soviet Union in the decades after World War II is usually characterized as one of
   a. limited war.
   b. contained war.
   c. détente.
   d. cold war.

9. Which of the following nations was among the first Eastern European nations to be invited to become a full-fledged member of an expanded NATO?
   a. Bosnia
   b. Hungary
   c. Serbia
   d. Russia

10. The approach to foreign policy that explicitly served to scale back U.S. overseas commitments by linking commitments to interests was the
    a. Monroe Doctrine.
    b. Truman Doctrine.
    c. Carter Doctrine.
    d. Nixon Doctrine.

11. Which is *not* true of the International Liberals?
    a. They use international government to protect the environment.
    b. They use international government to improve conditions of workers.
    c. They use international government to aid children in foreign countries.
    d. They use international government to provide subsidies to national businesses.

12. Which of the following is a foreign policy power explicitly assigned to the president under the Constitution?
    a. The power to declare war
    b. The power to receive ambassadors
    c. The power to conclude executive agreements
    d. All of the above

13. Which of these institutions was *not* established as part of the post-World War II reorganization of the foreign and defense policy apparatus?
    a. The Department of State
    b. The Department of Defense
    c. The National Security Council
    d. The Central Intelligence Agency

14. Based on the chapter's opening vignette, Senator Jesse Helms is an example of an
    a. International Liberal.
    b. International Conservative.
    c. International Libertarian.
    d. International Communitarian.

15. Newer research on public opinion suggests that where foreign policy is concerned, the public
    a. is better informed than it is on domestic issues.
    b. is able to reach consensus on preferred policy alternatives.
    c. maintains underlying attitudes that are stable, though more changeable than their opinions on domestic matters.
    d. consistently supports long-term military commitments.

16. A policy pronouncement that clearly identified the Persian Gulf as vitally important to U.S. interests was the
    a. Carter Doctrine.
    b. Monroe Doctrine.
    c. Nixon Doctrine.
    d. Ford Doctrine.

17. The Clinton administration replaced the Cold War policy of containment with a policy of
    a. constructive disengagement.
    b. enlargement and engagement.
    c. détente and peace.
    d. cooperation.

18. Under the Constitution, Congress has the power to
    a. take command of the Army.
    b. raise, support, and maintain the Navy.
    c. approve executive agreements.
    d. receive ambassadors.

19. The War Powers Resolution
    a. has been popular with presidents, who believe it increases their power.
    b. has been invoked frequently to limit the president's foreign policy actions.
    c. has been declared unconstitutional.
    d. allows a president to commit troops for 60 days without congressional approval.

20. Where foreign policy matters are concerned, interest groups
    a. provide the Department of State with a strong, built-in constituency.
    b. are more effective in noncrisis situations than in crisis situations.
    c. are more effective at bringing about change than at supporting the status quo.
    d. are prohibited from forming where national security matters are at stake.

21. Which of the following is *true* concerning a pact between the heads of two countries?
    a. It requires ratification by the Senate.
    b. It is outside the range of presidential power.
    c. It may have the legal status of a treaty.
    d. None of the above.

22. In April of 1997, the U.S. Senate ratified
    a. the Kyoto agreement.
    b. the Chemical Weapons Convention.
    c. NAFTA.
    d. the Biodiversity Treaty.

23. A liberal trade regime emphasizes
    a. global equality through income redistribution programs.
    b. managed trade.
    c. free trade.
    d. big government and extensive regulation.

24. Which is *not* true for the International Conservatives?
    a. They favor spending for national defense.
    b. They favor support of U.S. intelligence agencies.
    c. They favor placing U.S. forces under command of international organizations.
    d. They favor using the military only to fight in defense of vital national interests.

25. The most recent treaty rejected by the Senate is the
    a. ABM Treaty.
    b. Comprehensive Test Ban Treaty.
    c. SALT I Treaty.
    d. NAFTA Treaty.

Essay Questions

1. How has the emergence of new democracies in Russia and Eastern Europe affected basic assumptions guiding U.S. foreign policy?

2. What fundamental changes in American foreign and defense policy came about as part of the aftermath of World War II?

3. Discuss détente as a strategy of containment. How well did it work?

4. How has the increased emphasis on "low politics" changed traditional ways of thinking and acting in American foreign policy?

5. What role should the United States play in major global issues?

Answers to Multiple-Choice Questions

Chapter 1

1.	d	10.	a	19.	c
2.	b	11.	a	20.	d
3.	a	12.	b	21.	d
4.	c	13.	d	22.	a
5.	b	14.	c	23.	a
6.	c	15.	a	24.	d
7.	d	16.	b	25.	c
8.	b	17.	c		
9.	c	18.	d		

Chapter 2

1.	a	10.	c	19.	b
2.	a	11.	b	20.	d
3.	c	12.	a	21.	a
4.	d	13.	b	22.	a
5.	d	14.	c	23.	d
6.	a	15.	b	24.	b
7.	a	16.	c	25.	d
8.	c	17.	a		
9.	c	18.	b		

Chapter 3

1.	b	10.	c	19.	b
2.	a	11.	c	20.	d
3.	c	12.	a	21.	c
4.	c	13.	d	22.	d
5.	c	14.	c	23.	c
6.	a	15.	d	24.	a
7.	d	16.	d	25.	d
8.	a	17.	b		
9.	b	18.	c		

Chapter 4

1. c	10. b	19. c
2. a	11. d	20. d
3. a	12. b	21. c
4. b	13. a	22. c
5. a	14. a	23. d
6. c	15. c	24. b
7. d	16. b	25. a
8. a	17. d	
9. a	18. a	

Chapter 5

1. c	10. a	19. c
2. a	11. a	20. ?
3. b	12. ?	21. c
4. d	13. d	22. a
5. a	14. b	23. d
6. a	15. b	24. c
7. b	16. b	25. b
8. b	17. d	
9. d	18. c	

Chapter 6

1. a	10. a	19. a
2. c	11. d	20. a
3. b	12. c	21. a
4. a	13. a	22. a
5. b	14. c	23. b
6. b	15. c	24. a
7. c	16. b	25. d
8. d	17. a	
9. b	18. b	

Chapter 7

1.	b	10.	d	19.	c
2.	d	11.	c	20.	c
3.	c	12.	a	21.	c
4.	d	13.	a	22.	b
5.	a	14.	d	23.	a
6.	b	15.	a	24.	b
7.	b	16.	a	25.	d
8.	b	17.	a		
9.	a	18.	d		

Chapter 8

1.	c	10.	b	19.	d
2.	b	11.	d	20.	a
3.	c	12.	b	21.	d
4.	b	13.	c	22.	c
5.	c	14.	d	23.	b
6.	c	15.	a	24.	b
7.	a	16.	c	25.	d
8.	c	17.	a		
9.	b	18.	a		

Chapter 9

1.	c	10.	c	19.	c
2.	d	11.	d	20.	d
3.	b	12.	a	21.	a
4.	c	13.	c	22.	c
5.	c	14.	c	23.	c
6.	d	15.	a	24.	a
7.	a	16.	a	25.	b
8.	c	17.	c		
9.	b	18.	d		

Chapter 10

1. c	10. a	19. a
2. b	11. a	20. b
3. a	12. a	21. a
4. b	13. a	22. b
5. d	14. b	23. b
6. a	15. c	24. d
7. c	16. c	25. d
8. a	17. d	
9. a	18. c	

Chapter 11

1. a	10. b	19. a
2. b	11. c	20. c
3. a	12. d	21. d
4. c	13. a	22. a
5. a	14. b	23. a
6. d	15. d	24. a
7. a	16. b	25. d
8. d	17. d	
9. b	18. d	

Chapter 12

1. c	10. a	19. a
2. b	11. b	20. a
3. a	12. b	21. c
4. b	13. b	22. a
5. a	14. a	23. b
6. c	15. c	24. b
7. c	16. c	25. d
8. c	17. d	
9. b	18. d	

Chapter 13

1. a	10. a	19. c
2. d	11. b	20. a
3. c	12. b	21. d
4. a	13. b	22. d
5. b	14. d	23. b
6. c	15. d	24. d
7. a	16. a	25. b
8. a	17. a	
9. b	18. d	

Chapter 14

1. d	10. a	19. d
2. a	11. b	20. d
3. a	12. d	21. a
4. a	13. c	22. d
5. a	14. b	23. d
6. c	15. b	24. a
7. b	16. b	25. d
8. a	17. c	
9. b	18. b	

Chapter 15

1. a	10. a	19. c
2. b	11. c	20. d
3. a	12. a	21. b
4. d	13. c	22. c
5. b	14. b	23. a
6. b	15. b	24. a
7. a	16. c	25. a
8. c	17. d	
9. a	18. c	

Chapter 16

1. b	10. d	19. a
2. b	11. d	20. b
3. a	12. c	21. d
4. c	13. b	22. a
5. b	14. a	23. d
6. a	15. a	24. b
7. c	16. c	25. b
8. b	17. d	
9. b	18. a	

Chapter 17

1. b	10. c	19. d
2. a	11. b	20. c
3. c	12. a	21. c
4. c	13. a	22. c
5. c	14. a	23. d
6. b	15. c	24. b
7. a	16. d	25. b
8. a	17. d	
9. a	18. a	

Chapter 18

1. a	10. b	19. c
2. a	11. d	20. c
3. a	12. b	21. c
4. b	13. c	22. d
5. c	14. c	23. d
6. c	15. a	24. d
7. d	16. a	25. c
8. b	17. b	
9. d	18. d	

Chapter 19

1. b	10. b	19. a
2. d	11. d	20. b
3. d	12. c	21. d
4. d	13. a	22. c
5. c	14. b	23. c
6. d	15. c	24. d
7. b	16. b	25. b
8. d	17. a	
9. d	18. b	

Chapter 20

1. d	10. d	19. d
2. c	11. d	20. b
3. b	12. b	21. c
4. a	13. a	22. b
5. b	14. b	23. c
6. b	15. c	24. c
7. c	16. a	25. b
8. d	17. b	
9. b	18. b